MznLnx

Missing Links Exam Preps

Exam Prep for

Marketing Research Essentials

McDaniel, Jr. & Gates, 5th Edition

The MznLnx Exam Prep is your link from the texbook and lecture to your exams.
The MznLnx Exam Preps are unauthorized and comprehensive reviews of your textbooks.

All material provided by MznLnx and Rico Publications (c) 2010
Textbook publishers and textbook authors do not particpate in or contribute to these reviews.

MznLnx

Rico Publications

Exam Prep for Marketing Research Essentials
5th Edition
McDaniel, Jr. & Gates

Publisher: Raymond Houge
Assistant Editor: Michael Rouger
Text and Cover Designer: Lisa Buckner
Marketing Manager: Sara Swagger
Project Manager, Editorial Production: Jerry Emerson
Art Director: Vernon Lowerui

Product Manager: Dave Mason
Editorial Assitant: Rachel Guzmanji
Pedagogy: Debra Long
Cover Image: Jim Reed/Getty Images
Text and Cover Printer: City Printing, Inc.
Compositor: Media Mix, Inc.

(c) 2010 Rico Publications

ALL RIGHTS RESERVED. No part of this work covered by the copyright may be reproduced or used in any form or by an means--graphic, electronic, or mechanical, including photocopying, recording, taping, Web distribution, information storage, and retrieval systems, or in any other manner--without the written permission of the publisher.

For more information about our products, contact us at:
Dave.Mason@RicoPublications.com

For permission to use material from this text or product, submit a request online to:
Dave.Mason@RicoPublications.com

Printed in the United States
ISBN:

Contents

CHAPTER 1
The Role of Marketing Research in Decision Making — 1

CHAPTER 2
Problem Definition and the Research Process — 7

CHAPTER 3
Secondary Data and Databases — 14

CHAPTER 4
Qualitative Research — 22

CHAPTER 5
Survey Research: The Profound Impact of the Internet — 28

CHAPTER 6
Primary Data Collection: Observation — 38

CHAPTER 7
Primary Data Collection: Experimentation — 46

CHAPTER 8
The Concept of Measurement — 54

CHAPTER 9
Questionnaire Design — 62

CHAPTER 10
Basic Sampling Issues — 68

CHAPTER 11
Sample Size Determination — 71

CHAPTER 12
Data Processing and Fundamental Data Analysis — 77

CHAPTER 13
Bivariate Correlation and Regression — 84

CHAPTER 14
Communicating the Research Results — 88

CHAPTER 15
Managing Marketing Research and Research Ethics — 91

ANSWER KEY — 97

TO THE STUDENT

COMPREHENSIVE

The *MznLnx* Exam Prep series is designed to help you pass your exams. Editors at MznLnx review your textbooks and then prepare these practice exams to help you master the textbook material. Unlike study guides, workbooks, and practice tests provided by the texbook publisher and textbook authors, *MznLnx* gives you **all** of the material in each chapter in exam form, not just samples, so you can be sure to nail your exam.

MECHANICAL

The MznLnx Exam Prep series creates exams that will help you learn the subject matter as well as test you on your understanding. Each question is designed to help you master the concept. Just working through the exams, you gain an understanding of the subject--its a simple mechanical process that produces success.

INTEGRATED STUDY GUIDE AND REVIEW

MznLnx is not just a set of exams designed to test you, its also a comprehensive review of the subject content. Each exam question is also a review of the concept, making sure that you will get the answer correct without having to go to other sources of material. You learn as you go! Its the easiest way to pass an exam.

HUMOR

Studying can be tedious and dry. MznLnx's instructional design includes moderate humor within the exam questions on occassion, to break the tedium and revitalize the brain

Chapter 1. The Role of Marketing Research in Decision Making

1. _____ is a broad label that refers to any individuals or households that use goods and services generated within the economy. The concept of a _____ is used in different contexts, so that the usage and significance of the term may vary.

   A _____ is a person who uses any product or service.

   a. Power III
   b. Consumer
   c. 6-3-5 Brainwriting
   d. 180SearchAssistant

2. _____ is defined by the American _____ Association as the activity, set of institutions, and processes for creating, communicating, delivering, and exchanging offerings that have value for customers, clients, partners, and society at large. The term developed from the original meaning which referred literally to going to market, as in shopping, or going to a market to sell goods or services.

   _____ practice tends to be seen as a creative industry, which includes advertising, distribution and selling.

   a. Customer acquisition management
   b. Marketing myopia
   c. Product naming
   d. Marketing

3. The _____ is generally accepted as the use and specification of the four p's describing the strategic position of a product in the marketplace. One version of the origins of the _____ starts in 1948 when James Culliton said that a marketing decision should be a result of something similar to a recipe. This version continued in 1953 when Neil Borden, in his American Marketing Association presidential address, took the recipe idea one step further and coined the term 'Marketing-Mix'.

   a. 180SearchAssistant
   b. 6-3-5 Brainwriting
   c. Power III
   d. Marketing mix

4. The _____ is a professional association for marketers. As of 2008 it had approximately 40,000 members. There are collegiate chapters on 250 campuses.

   a. ACNielsen
   b. ADTECH
   c. American Marketing Association
   d. AMAX

Chapter 1. The Role of Marketing Research in Decision Making

5. Consumer market research is a form of applied sociology that concentrates on understanding the behaviours, whims and preferences, of consumers in a market-based economy, and aims to understand the effects and comparative success of marketing campaigns. The field of consumer _____ as a statistical science was pioneered by Arthur Nielsen with the founding of the ACNielsen Company in 1923.

Thus _____ is the systematic and objective identification, collection, analysis, and dissemination of information for the purpose of assisting management in decision making related to the identification and solution of problems and opportunities in marketing.

   a. Focus group
   b. Marketing research process
   c. Logit analysis
   d. Marketing research

6. _____ is either an activity of a living being (such as a human), consisting of receiving knowledge of the outside world through the senses, or the recording of data using scientific instruments. The term may also refer to any datum collected during this activity.

The scientific method requires _____s of nature to formulate and test hypotheses.

   a. ACNielsen
   b. ADTECH
   c. AMAX
   d. Observation

7. _____ a research method involving the use of questionnaires and/or statistical surveys to gather data about people and their thoughts and behaviours.
   a. Z-test
   b. Control chart
   c. Survey research
   d. T-test

8. In economics, an externality or spillover of an economic transaction is an impact on a party that is not directly involved in the transaction. In such a case, prices do not reflect the full costs or benefits in production or consumption of a product or service. A positive impact is called an _____ benefit, while a negative impact is called an _____ cost.

a. ACNielsen
b. ADTECH
c. AMAX
d. External

9. A _____ is a statement or claim that a particular event will occur in the future in more certain terms than a forecast. The etymology of this word is Latin . In regards to predicting the future Howard H. Stevenson Says, '_____ is at least two things: Important and hard.' Important, because we have to act, and hard because we have to realize the future we want, and what is the best way to get there.

a. Power III
b. 180SearchAssistant
c. Prediction
d. 6-3-5 Brainwriting

10. _____ is an advertisement in which a particular product specifically mentions a competitor by name for the express purpose of showing why the competitor is inferior to the product naming it.

This should not be confused with parody advertisements, where a fictional product is being advertised for the purpose of poking fun at the particular advertisement, nor should it be confused with the use of a coined brand name for the purpose of comparing the product without actually naming an actual competitor. ('Wikipedia tastes better and is less filling than the Encyclopedia Galactica.')

In the 1980s, during what has been referred to as the cola wars, soft-drink manufacturer Pepsi ran a series of advertisements where people, caught on hidden camera, in a blind taste test, chose Pepsi over rival Coca-Cola.

a. Comparative advertising
b. GL-70
c. Heavy-up
d. Cost per conversion

11. Bain is a Scottish surname. See Clan MacBain. Bain may also refer to:

- The River Bain in Lincolnshire, England
- The River Bain, North Yorkshire, England

- _____, management consulting firm
- Bain Capital, private equity group

- Donald III of Scotland, King of Scotland 1093-1097
- Sir. Stafford Bain JR, Former Prime Minister of the Bahamas

- Addison Bain
- Alexander Bain, Scottish philosopher and educationalist
- Alexander Bain (inventor)
- Aly Bain
- Andrew Geddes Bain
- Atu Emberson Bain
- Barbara Bain
- Bill Bain, founder of _____
- Bonar Bain
- Conrad Bain
- Dan Bain
- David Bain
- Donald Bain:
    - Donald Bain (writer)
- Edgar Bain, metallurgist
- Ewen Bain
- F. W. Bain
- George Bain:
    - George Bain (academic)
    - George Bain (journalist) (1920-2006), Canadian journalist
    - George Grantham Bain (1865-1944) New Yorker news photographer
- James Thompson Bain
- Jimmy Bain
- Joe S. Bain (1912-1991) American economist
- Mary Monnett Bain
- Raymone Bain
- Sam Bain
- Thomas Bain
- Jeffery Scott Bain Environment, Safety ' Health Professional

- Bain (Middle-earth), King of Dale in Middle-earth
- Bain (Wheel of Time), a Maiden of the Spear from the Wheel of Time series.
- Sunset Bain, character in the Marvel Comics universe
- Sheriff Joe Bain
- Miguel Bain, a character in the 1995 film Assassins, portrayed by Antonio Banderas

a. 180SearchAssistant
b. Bain ' Company
c. Power III
d. 6-3-5 Brainwriting

12. A _____ is a process that can allow an organization to concentrate its limited resources on the greatest opportunities to increase sales and achieve a sustainable competitive advantage. A _____ should be centered around the key concept that customer satisfaction is the main goal.

A _____ is most effective when it is an integral component of corporate strategy, defining how the organization will successfully engage customers, prospects, and competitors in the market arena.

a. Psychographic
b. Societal marketing
c. Cyberdoc
d. Marketing strategy

13. A _____ is a plan of action designed to achieve a particular goal.

_____ is different from tactics. In military terms, tactics is concerned with the conduct of an engagement while _____ is concerned with how different engagements are linked.

a. 180SearchAssistant
b. Strategy
c. 6-3-5 Brainwriting
d. Power III

14. _____, fundamental research (sometimes pure research), is research carried out to increase understanding of fundamental principles. Many times the end results have no direct or immediate commercial benefits, which is to say that _____ can be thought of as arising out of pure curiosity. However, in the long term it is the basis for many commercial products and applied research.

a. Reference value
b. Power III
c. Response rate
d. Basic research

15. Procter is a surname, and may also refer to:

- Bryan Waller Procter (pseud. Barry Cornwall), English poet
- Goodwin Procter, American law firm
- _____, consumer products multinational

a. Procter ' Gamble
b. Convergent
c. Black PRies
d. Flyer

16. _____, also referred to as i-marketing, web marketing, online marketing is the marketing of products or services over the Internet.

The Internet has brought many unique benefits to marketing, one of which being lower costs for the distribution of information and media to a global audience. The interactive nature of _____, both in terms of providing instant response and eliciting responses, is a unique quality of the medium.

a. ACNielsen
b. AMAX
c. ADTECH
d. Internet Marketing

17. _____s are used in open sentences. For instance, in the formula x + 1 = 5, x is a _____ which represents an 'unknown' number. _____s are often represented by letters of the Roman alphabet, or those of other alphabets, such as Greek, and use other special symbols.

a. Quantitative
b. Variable
c. Book of business
d. Personalization

Chapter 2. Problem Definition and the Research Process

1. _____ is defined by the American _____ Association as the activity, set of institutions, and processes for creating, communicating, delivering, and exchanging offerings that have value for customers, clients, partners, and society at large. The term developed from the original meaning which referred literally to going to market, as in shopping, or going to a market to sell goods or services.

   _____ practice tends to be seen as a creative industry, which includes advertising, distribution and selling.

   a. Marketing
   b. Customer acquisition management
   c. Product naming
   d. Marketing myopia

2. Consumer market research is a form of applied sociology that concentrates on understanding the behaviours, whims and preferences, of consumers in a market-based economy, and aims to understand the effects and comparative success of marketing campaigns. The field of consumer _____ as a statistical science was pioneered by Arthur Nielsen with the founding of the ACNielsen Company in 1923.

   Thus _____ is the systematic and objective identification, collection, analysis, and dissemination of information for the purpose of assisting management in decision making related to the identification and solution of problems and opportunities in marketing.

   a. Logit analysis
   b. Marketing research
   c. Marketing research process
   d. Focus group

3. _____ is either an activity of a living being (such as a human), consisting of receiving knowledge of the outside world through the senses, or the recording of data using scientific instruments. The term may also refer to any datum collected during this activity.

   The scientific method requires _____s of nature to formulate and test hypotheses.

   a. ACNielsen
   b. ADTECH
   c. AMAX
   d. Observation

4. _____ a research method involving the use of questionnaires and/or statistical surveys to gather data about people and their thoughts and behaviours.

Chapter 2. Problem Definition and the Research Process

a. Z-test
b. Survey research
c. T-test
d. Control chart

5. _____ is a type of research conducted because a problem has not been clearly defined. _____ helps determine the best research design, data collection method and selection of subjects. Given its fundamental nature, _____ often concludes that a perceived problem does not actually exist.

a. ACNielsen
b. IDDEA
c. Intent scale translation
d. Exploratory research

6. _____ is a marketing term, and involves evaluating the situation and trends in a particular company's market. _____ is often called the 'three c's', which refers to the three major elements that must be studied:

- Customers
- Costs
- Competition

The number of 'c's' is sometimes extended to four, five, or even six, with 'Collaboration', 'Company', and 'Competitive advantage'.

- Marketing mix
- SWOT analysis

a. Situation analysis
b. 180SearchAssistant
c. Power III
d. 6-3-5 Brainwriting

Chapter 2. Problem Definition and the Research Process

7. A number of different _____s are indicated below.

- Randomized controlled trial
    - Double-blind randomized trial
    - Single-blind randomized trial
    - Non-blind trial
- Nonrandomized trial (quasi-experiment)
    - Interrupted time series design (measures on a sample or a series of samples from the same population are obtained several times before and after a manipulated event or a naturally occurring event) - considered a type of quasi-experiment

- Cohort study
    - Prospective cohort
    - Retrospective cohort
    - Time series study
- Case-control study
    - Nested case-control study
- Cross-sectional study
    - Community survey (a type of cross-sectional study)

When choosing a _____, many factors must be taken into account. Different types of studies are subject to different types of bias. For example, recall bias is likely to occur in cross-sectional or case-control studies where subjects are asked to recall exposure to risk factors.

a. 180SearchAssistant
b. Study design
c. Power III
d. Longitudinal studies

8. _____s are used in open sentences. For instance, in the formula $x + 1 = 5$, x is a _____ which represents an 'unknown' number. _____s are often represented by letters of the Roman alphabet, or those of other alphabets, such as Greek, and use other special symbols.

a. Quantitative
b. Book of business
c. Personalization
d. Variable

9. The terms '_____' and 'independent variable' are used in similar but subtly different ways in mathematics and statistics as part of the standard terminology in those subjects. They are used to distinguish between two types of quantities being considered, separating them into those available at the start of a process and those being created by it, where the latter (_____s) are dependent on the former (independent variables.)

Chapter 2. Problem Definition and the Research Process

In traditional calculus, a function is defined as a relation between two terms called variables because their values vary.

a. Field experiment
b. 180SearchAssistant
c. Dependent variable
d. Power III

10. _____ is a global marketing research firm, with worldwide headquarters in New York City. Regional headquarters for North America are located in Schaumburg, IL. As of 2008, its the part of The Nielsen Company.
    a. E-Detailing
    b. Alloy Entertainment
    c. InfoNU
    d. ACNielsen

11. _____ are used to collect quantitative information about items in a population. Surveys of human populations and institutions are common in political polling and government, health, social science and marketing research. A survey may focus on opinions or factual information depending on its purpose, and many surveys involve administering questions to individuals.
    a. Gross Margin Return on Inventory Investment
    b. Statistical surveys
    c. BeyondROI
    d. Convergent

12. A _____ is a research instrument consisting of a series of questions and other prompts for the purpose of gathering information from respondents. Although they are often designed for statistical analysis of the responses, this is not always the case. The _____ was invented by Sir Francis Galton.
    a. Questionnaire
    b. Market research
    c. Mystery shoppers
    d. Mystery shopping

13. _____, fundamental research (sometimes pure research), is research carried out to increase understanding of fundamental principles. Many times the end results have no direct or immediate commercial benefits, which is to say that _____ can be thought of as arising out of pure curiosity. However, in the long term it is the basis for many commercial products and applied research.

Chapter 2. Problem Definition and the Research Process

a. Reference value
b. Basic research
c. Response rate
d. Power III

14. In engineering and manufacturing, _____ is involved in developing systems to ensure products or services are designed and produced to meet or exceed customer requirements or SLA's. Genetic algorithms are search techniques, used in computing to find exact or approximate solutions to optimization and search problems.

Alternative _____ procedures can be applied on a process to test statistically the null hypothesis, that the process is in control, against the alternative, that the process is out of control.

a. 180SearchAssistant
b. 6-3-5 Brainwriting
c. Power III
d. Quality control

15. The '_____' is an expression which typically refers to the theory of scale types developed by the Harvard psychologist Stanley Smith Stevens In this article Stevens claimed that all measurement in science was conducted using four different types of numerical scales which he called 'nominal', 'ordinal', 'interval' and 'ratio'.

a. 6-3-5 Brainwriting
b. Levels of measurement
c. Power III
d. 180SearchAssistant

16. _____ is a way of expressing knowledge or belief that an event will occur or has occurred. In mathematics the concept has been given an exact meaning in _____ theory, that is used extensively in such areas of study as mathematics, statistics, finance, gambling, science, and philosophy to draw conclusions about the likelihood of potential events and the underlying mechanics of complex systems.

a. Linear regression
b. Data
c. Heteroskedastic
d. Probability

17. A sample is a subject chosen from a population for investigation. A _____ is one chosen by a method involving an unpredictable component. Random sampling can also refer to taking a number of independent observations from the same probability distribution, without involving any real population.

a. Random sample
b. Selection bias
c. 180SearchAssistant
d. Power III

18. _____ is that part of statistical practice concerned with the selection of individual observations intended to yield some knowledge about a population of concern, especially for the purposes of statistical inference. Each observation measures one or more properties (weight, location, etc.) of an observable entity enumerated to distinguish objects or individuals.
a. Sports Marketing Group
b. Sampling
c. AStore
d. Richard Buckminster 'Bucky' Fuller

19. _____ is a branch of philosophy which seeks to address questions about morality, such as how a moral outcome can be achieved in a specific situation (applied _____), how moral values should be determined (normative _____), what moral values people actually abide by (descriptive _____), what the fundamental semantic, ontological, and epistemic nature of _____ or morality is (meta-_____), and how moral capacity or moral agency develops and what its nature is (moral psychology.)

Socrates was one of the first Greek philosophers to encourage both scholars and the common citizen to turn their attention from the outside world to the condition of man. In this view, Knowledge having a bearing on human life was placed highest, all other knowledge being secondary.

a. ADTECH
b. AMAX
c. ACNielsen
d. Ethics

20. A _____ or subscription radio is a digital radio signal that is broadcast by a communications satellite, which covers a much wider geographical range than terrestrial radio signals.

For now, _____ offers a meaningful alternative to ground-based radio services in some countries, notably the United States. Mobile services, such as Sirius, XM, and Worldspace, allow listeners to roam across an entire continent, listening to the same audio programming anywhere they go.

a. 180SearchAssistant
b. 6-3-5 Brainwriting
c. Power III
d. Satellite radio

Chapter 3. Secondary Data and Databases

1. _____ is a term for unprocessed data, it is also known as primary data. It is a relative term _____ can be input to a computer program or used in manual analysis procedures such as gathering statistics from a survey.
    a. Product manager
    b. Chief marketing officer
    c. Shoppers Food ' Pharmacy
    d. Raw data

2. Combining Existing _____ Sources with New Primary Data Sources

Imagine that we could get hold of a good collection of surveys taken in earlier years, such as detailed studies about changes going on in this phase and hopefully additional studies in the years to come. Analyzing this data base over time could give us a good picture of what changes actually have taken place in the orientation of the population and of the extent to which new technical concepts did have an impact on subgroups of the population. Furthermore, data archives can help to prepare studies on change over time by monitoring what questions have been asked in earlier years and alerting principal investigators to important questions which should be repeated in planned research projects.

    a. Power III
    b. Secondary data
    c. 180SearchAssistant
    d. 6-3-5 Brainwriting

3. _____ refer to a collection of facts usually collected as the result of experience, observation or experiment or a set of premises. This may consist of numbers, words particularly as measurements or observations of a set of variables. _____ are often viewed as a lowest level of abstraction from which information and knowledge are derived.
    a. Pearson product-moment correlation coefficient
    b. Data
    c. Mean
    d. Sample size

4. A _____ is a structured collection of records or data that is stored in a computer system. The structure is achieved by organizing the data according to a _____ model. The model in most common use today is the relational model.
    a. 6-3-5 Brainwriting
    b. 180SearchAssistant
    c. Power III
    d. Database

Chapter 3. Secondary Data and Databases

5. _____ is a form of direct marketing using databases of customers or potential customers to generate personalized communications in order to promote a product or service for marketing purposes. The method of communication can be any addressable medium, as in direct marketing.

The distinction between direct and _____ stems primarily from the attention paid to the analysis of data.

   a. Power III
   b. Direct marketing
   c. Direct Marketing Associations
   d. Database marketing

6. _____ is defined by the American _____ Association as the activity, set of institutions, and processes for creating, communicating, delivering, and exchanging offerings that have value for customers, clients, partners, and society at large. The term developed from the original meaning which referred literally to going to market, as in shopping, or going to a market to sell goods or services.

_____ practice tends to be seen as a creative industry, which includes advertising, distribution and selling.

   a. Product naming
   b. Marketing myopia
   c. Customer acquisition management
   d. Marketing

7. The _____ is generally accepted as the use and specification of the four p's describing the strategic position of a product in the marketplace. One version of the origins of the _____ starts in 1948 when James Culliton said that a marketing decision should be a result of something similar to a recipe. This version continued in 1953 when Neil Borden, in his American Marketing Association presidential address, took the recipe idea one step further and coined the term 'Marketing-Mix'.

   a. 6-3-5 Brainwriting
   b. Power III
   c. 180SearchAssistant
   d. Marketing mix

8. _____ is a type of advertising whereby advertisements are placed so as to reach consumers based on various traits such as demographics, purchase history, or observed behavior.

Two principal forms of targeted interactive advertising are behavioral targeting and contextual advertising.

Chapter 3. Secondary Data and Databases

a. Targeted advertising
b. Brand parity
c. Sugging
d. Specialty catalogs

9. _____ is the process of extracting hidden patterns from data. As more data is gathered, with the amount of data doubling every three years, _____ is becoming an increasingly important tool to transform this data into information. It is commonly used in a wide range of profiling practices, such as marketing, surveillance, fraud detection and scientific discovery.
   a. Structure mining
   b. Power III
   c. 180SearchAssistant
   d. Data mining

10. Traditionally, the term _____ had been used to refer to a network or circuit of biological neurons. The modern usage of the term often refers to artificial _____s, which are composed of artificial neurons or nodes. Thus the term has two distinct usages:

    1. Biological _____s are made up of real biological neurons that are connected or functionally related in the peripheral nervous system or the central nervous system. In the field of neuroscience, they are often identified as groups of neurons that perform a specific physiological function in laboratory analysis.
    2. Artificial _____s are made up of interconnecting artificial neurons (programming constructs that mimic the properties of biological neurons.) Artificial _____s may either be used to gain an understanding of biological _____s, or for solving artificial intelligence problems without necessarily creating a model of a real biological system. The real, biological nervous system is highly complex and includes some features that may seem superfluous based on an understanding of artificial networks

    In general a biological _____ is composed of a group or groups of chemically connected or functionally associated neurons.

   a. 6-3-5 Brainwriting
   b. Neural network
   c. Power III
   d. 180SearchAssistant

11. The _____ is an independent agency of the United States government, established in 1914 by the _____ Act. Its principal mission is the promotion of 'consumer protection' and the elimination and prevention of what regulators perceive to be harmfully 'anti-competitive' business practices, such as coercive monopoly.

    The _____ Act was one of President Wilson's major acts against trusts.

Chapter 3. Secondary Data and Databases

a. 6-3-5 Brainwriting
b. Federal Trade Commission
c. 180SearchAssistant
d. Power III

12. _____ is either an activity of a living being (such as a human), consisting of receiving knowledge of the outside world through the senses, or the recording of data using scientific instruments. The term may also refer to any datum collected during this activity.

The scientific method requires _____s of nature to formulate and test hypotheses.

a. ADTECH
b. AMAX
c. ACNielsen
d. Observation

13. _____ is the ability of an individual or group to seclude themselves or information about themselves and thereby reveal themselves selectively. The boundaries and content of what is considered private differ among cultures and individuals, but share basic common themes. _____ is sometimes related to anonymity, the wish to remain unnoticed or unidentified in the public realm.
a. 6-3-5 Brainwriting
b. Power III
c. Privacy
d. 180SearchAssistant

14. _____ a research method involving the use of questionnaires and/or statistical surveys to gather data about people and their thoughts and behaviours.
a. Survey research
b. T-test
c. Z-test
d. Control chart

15. _____ is a broad label that refers to any individuals or households that use goods and services generated within the economy. The concept of a _____ is used in different contexts, so that the usage and significance of the term may vary.

A _____ is a person who uses any product or service.

a. Power III
b. 180SearchAssistant
c. 6-3-5 Brainwriting
d. Consumer

16. Consumer market research is a form of applied sociology that concentrates on understanding the behaviours, whims and preferences, of consumers in a market-based economy, and aims to understand the effects and comparative success of marketing campaigns. The field of consumer _____ as a statistical science was pioneered by Arthur Nielsen with the founding of the ACNielsen Company in 1923.

Thus _____ is the systematic and objective identification, collection, analysis, and dissemination of information for the purpose of assisting management in decision making related to the identification and solution of problems and opportunities in marketing.

a. Marketing research
b. Focus group
c. Logit analysis
d. Marketing research process

17. Though criteria for causality in statistical studies have been researched intensely, Pearl has shown that _____ cannot be defined in terms of statistical notions alone; some causal assumptions are necessary. In a 1965 paper, Austin Bradford Hill proposed a set of causal criteria.. Many working epidemiologists take these as a good place to start when considering confounding and causation.
a. Confounding variables
b. Survey research
c. T-test
d. Linear regression

18. _____ is a popular searchable archive of content from newspapers, magazines, legal documents and other printed sources. _____ claims to be the 'world's largest collection of public records, unpublished opinions, forms, legal, news, and business information' while offering their products to a wide range of professionals in the legal, risk management, corporate, government, law enforcement, accounting and academic markets. Typical customers of _____ include lawyers, law students, journalists, and academics.
a. LexisNexis
b. 180SearchAssistant
c. Power III
d. 6-3-5 Brainwriting

Chapter 3. Secondary Data and Databases

19. A _____ is a repository usually within the Usenet system, for messages posted from many users in different locations. The term may be confusing to some, because it is usually a discussion group. _____s are technically distinct from, but functionally similar to, discussion forums on the World Wide Web.
    a. 6-3-5 Brainwriting
    b. Newsgroup
    c. Power III
    d. 180SearchAssistant

20. _____s are used in open sentences. For instance, in the formula x + 1 = 5, x is a _____ which represents an 'unknown' number. _____s are often represented by letters of the Roman alphabet, or those of other alphabets, such as Greek, and use other special symbols.
    a. Variable
    b. Personalization
    c. Book of business
    d. Quantitative

21. infoGROUP, formerly _____, is a provider of both business and consumer information and marketing solutions, which consists of data processing, database management and email marketing. InfoGroup is a publicly traded company since 1992 on the NASDAQ stock exchange under the ticker symbol IUSA. infoGROUP has over 4 million customers worldwide and revenues in 2006 were over $700 million.
    a. Adidas
    b. InfoUSA
    c. Amoco Corporation
    d. Eastman Kodak Company

22. _____ is the collection and management of information from one or more sources and the distribution of that information to one or more audiences. This sometimes involves those who have a stake in, or a right to that information. Management means the organization of and control over the structure, processing and delivery of information.
    a. Information management
    b. ADTECH
    c. AMAX
    d. ACNielsen

23. _____ is the study of the Earth and its lands, features, inhabitants, and phenomena. A literal translation would be 'to describe or write about the Earth'. The first person to use the word '_____' was Eratosthenes .

Chapter 3. Secondary Data and Databases

a. Power III
b. 6-3-5 Brainwriting
c. 180SearchAssistant
d. Geography

24. A _____ captures, stores, analyzes, manages, and presents data that is linked to location.

In the strictest sense, the term describes any information system that integrates, stores, edits, analyzes, shares, and displays geographic information. In a more generic sense, _____ applications are tools that allow users to create interactive queries (user created searches), analyze spatial information, edit data, maps, and present the results of all these operations.

a. Geographic information system
b. Power III
c. 6-3-5 Brainwriting
d. 180SearchAssistant

25. _____ constitute a class of computer-based information systems including knowledge-based systems that support decision-making activities.

_____ are a specific class of computerized information system that supports business and organizational decision-making activities. A properly-designed _____ is an interactive software-based system intended to help decision makers compile useful information from raw data, documents, personal knowledge, and/or business models to identify and solve problems and make decisions.

a. Decision support systems
b. 180SearchAssistant
c. Power III
d. 6-3-5 Brainwriting

26.

_____ was founded in 1986 by Laszlo Bardos, Andrew Dressel, John Haller, Mike Marvin, and Sean O'Sullivan. The company originated as a Rensselaer Polytechnic Institute (RPI) incubator project. The original name was Navigational Technologies Incorporated (NTI), and the first intended product was for in-car navigation.

a. Mapinfo
b. Consumers Union
c. Multinational corporation
d. VideoJug

Chapter 4. Qualitative Research

1. A _____ is a form of qualitative research in which a group of people are asked about their attitude towards a product, service, concept, advertisement, idea, or packaging. Questions are asked in an interactive group setting where participants are free to talk with other group members.

   Ernest Dichter originated the idea of having a 'group therapy' for products and this process is what became known as a _____.

   a. Logit analysis
   b. Focus group
   c. Marketing research process
   d. Cross tabulation

2. _____ is a field of inquiry that crosscuts disciplines and subject matters. _____ers aim to gather an in-depth understanding of human behavior and the reasons that govern such behavior. The discipline investigates the why and how of decision making, not just what, where, when.
   a. Qualitative research
   b. 6-3-5 Brainwriting
   c. Power III
   d. 180SearchAssistant

3. A _____ attribute is one that exists in a range of magnitudes, and can therefore be measured. Measurements of any particular _____ property are expressed as a specific quantity, referred to as a unit, multiplied by a number. Examples of physical quantities are distance, mass, and time.
   a. Dolly Dimples
   b. BeyondROI
   c. Quantitative
   d. Lifestyle city

4. A _____ is a research instrument consisting of a series of questions and other prompts for the purpose of gathering information from respondents. Although they are often designed for statistical analysis of the responses, this is not always the case. The _____ was invented by Sir Francis Galton.
   a. Market research
   b. Mystery shopping
   c. Mystery shoppers
   d. Questionnaire

Chapter 4. Qualitative Research

5. _____ is the study of groups, and also a general term for group processes. Relevant to the fields of psychology, sociology, and communication studies, a group is two or more individuals who are connected to each other by social relationships. Because they interact and influence each other, groups develop a number of dynamic processes that separate them from a random collection of individuals.

   a. Power III
   b. Group dynamics
   c. 180SearchAssistant
   d. 6-3-5 Brainwriting

6. _____ is a form of communication that typically attempts to persuade potential customers to purchase or to consume more of a particular brand of product or service. 'While now central to the contemporary global economy and the reproduction of global production networks, it is only quite recently that _____ has been more than a marginal influence on patterns of sales and production. The formation of modern _____ was intimately bound up with the emergence of new forms of monopoly capitalism around the end of the 19th and beginning of the 20th century as one element in corporate strategies to create, organize and where possible control markets, especially for mass produced consumer goods.

   a. AMAX
   b. Advertising
   c. ACNielsen
   d. ADTECH

7. _____s are used in open sentences. For instance, in the formula x + 1 = 5, x is a _____ which represents an 'unknown' number. _____s are often represented by letters of the Roman alphabet, or those of other alphabets, such as Greek, and use other special symbols.

   a. Variable
   b. Quantitative
   c. Book of business
   d. Personalization

8. An _____ is one type of focus group, and is a sub-set of online research methods.

   A moderator invites prescreened, qualified respondents who represent the target of interest to log on to conferencing software at a pre-arranged time and to take part in an _____. Some researchers will offer incentives for participating but this raises a number of ethical questions.

   a. Online focus group
   b. Intangibility
   c. Automated surveys
   d. Engagement

Chapter 4. Qualitative Research

9. _____ is defined by the American _____ Association as the activity, set of institutions, and processes for creating, communicating, delivering, and exchanging offerings that have value for customers, clients, partners, and society at large. The term developed from the original meaning which referred literally to going to market, as in shopping, or going to a market to sell goods or services.

_____ practice tends to be seen as a creative industry, which includes advertising, distribution and selling.

  a. Marketing myopia
  b. Marketing
  c. Customer acquisition management
  d. Product naming

10. Consumer market research is a form of applied sociology that concentrates on understanding the behaviours, whims and preferences, of consumers in a market-based economy, and aims to understand the effects and comparative success of marketing campaigns. The field of consumer _____ as a statistical science was pioneered by Arthur Nielsen with the founding of the ACNielsen Company in 1923 .

Thus _____ is the systematic and objective identification, collection, analysis, and dissemination of information for the purpose of assisting management in decision making related to the identification and solution of problems and opportunities in marketing.

  a. Focus group
  b. Logit analysis
  c. Marketing research process
  d. Marketing research

11. The Oxford University Press defines _____ as 'marketing on a worldwide scale reconciling or taking commercial advantage of global operational differences, similarities and opportunities in order to meet global objectives.' Oxford University Press' Glossary of Marketing Terms.

Here are three reasons for the shift from domestic to _____ as given by the authors of the textbook, _____ Management--3rd Edition by Masaaki Kotabe and Kristiaan Helsen, 2004.

One of the product categories in which global competition has been easy to track is in U.S. automotive sales.

  a. Diversity marketing
  b. Guerrilla Marketing
  c. Global marketing
  d. Digital marketing

Chapter 4. Qualitative Research

12. _____ is either an activity of a living being (such as a human), consisting of receiving knowledge of the outside world through the senses, or the recording of data using scientific instruments. The term may also refer to any datum collected during this activity.

The scientific method requires _____s of nature to formulate and test hypotheses.

a. Observation
b. AMAX
c. ADTECH
d. ACNielsen

13. _____ a research method involving the use of questionnaires and/or statistical surveys to gather data about people and their thoughts and behaviours.
a. T-test
b. Control chart
c. Z-test
d. Survey research

14. Procter is a surname, and may also refer to:

- Bryan Waller Procter (pseud. Barry Cornwall), English poet
- Goodwin Procter, American law firm
- _____, consumer products multinational

a. Flyer
b. Black PRies
c. Procter ' Gamble
d. Convergent

15. _____ is an American marketing research and consulting firm based in Arlington, Texas. It also operates the American Consumer Opinion online panel, which is made up of over seven million people. .
a. Decision Analyst
b. Financial analyst
c. Power III
d. Chief executive officer

Chapter 4. Qualitative Research

16. _____ is an advertisement in which a particular product specifically mentions a competitor by name for the express purpose of showing why the competitor is inferior to the product naming it.

This should not be confused with parody advertisements, where a fictional product is being advertised for the purpose of poking fun at the particular advertisement, nor should it be confused with the use of a coined brand name for the purpose of comparing the product without actually naming an actual competitor. ('Wikipedia tastes better and is less filling than the Encyclopedia Galactica.')

In the 1980s, during what has been referred to as the cola wars, soft-drink manufacturer Pepsi ran a series of advertisements where people, caught on hidden camera, in a blind taste test, chose Pepsi over rival Coca-Cola.

   a. GL-70
   b. Heavy-up
   c. Cost per conversion
   d. Comparative advertising

17. A _____, in psychology, is a personality test designed to let a person respond to ambiguous stimuli, presumably revealing hidden emotions and internal conflicts. This is different from an 'objective test' in which responses are analyzed according to a universal standard (for example, a multiple choice exam.) The responses to _____s are content analyzed for meaning rather than being based on presuppositions about meaning, as is the case with objective tests.
   a. Projective test
   b. Power III
   c. 6-3-5 Brainwriting
   d. 180SearchAssistant

18. _____ are a class of semi-structured projective techniques. _____ typically provide respondents with beginnings of sentences, referred to as 'stems,' and respondents then complete the sentences in ways that are meaningful to them. The responses are believed to provide indications of attitudes, beliefs, motivations, or other mental states.
   a. Power III
   b. Response rate
   c. Reference value
   d. Sentence completion tests

19. _____ is a common word game involving an exchange of words that are associated together.

Once an original word has been chosen, usually randomly or arbitrarily, a player will find a word that they associate with it and make it known to all the players, usually by saying it aloud or writing it down as the next item on a list of words so far used. The next player must then do the same with this previous word.

Chapter 4. Qualitative Research

a. 180SearchAssistant
b. 6-3-5 Brainwriting
c. Power III
d. Word association

20. _____ is a broad label that refers to any individuals or households that use goods and services generated within the economy. The concept of a _____ is used in different contexts, so that the usage and significance of the term may vary.

A _____ is a person who uses any product or service.

a. 180SearchAssistant
b. Power III
c. 6-3-5 Brainwriting
d. Consumer

21. _____ is the conveying of events in words, images, and sounds often by improvisation or embellishment. Stories or narratives have been shared in every culture and in every land as a means of entertainment, education, preservation of culture and in order to instill moral values. Crucial elements of stories and _____ include plot and characters, as well as the narrative point of view.

a. Power III
b. 6-3-5 Brainwriting
c. Storytelling
d. 180SearchAssistant

Chapter 5. Survey Research: The Profound Impact of the Internet

1. _____ is a form of communication that typically attempts to persuade potential customers to purchase or to consume more of a particular brand of product or service. 'While now central to the contemporary global economy and the reproduction of global production networks, it is only quite recently that _____ has been more than a marginal influence on patterns of sales and production. The formation of modern _____ was intimately bound up with the emergence of new forms of monopoly capitalism around the end of the 19th and beginning of the 20th century as one element in corporate strategies to create, organize and where possible control markets, especially for mass produced consumer goods.
   a. ACNielsen
   b. ADTECH
   c. Advertising
   d. AMAX

2. _____ is defined by the American _____ Association as the activity, set of institutions, and processes for creating, communicating, delivering, and exchanging offerings that have value for customers, clients, partners, and society at large. The term developed from the original meaning which referred literally to going to market, as in shopping, or going to a market to sell goods or services.

   _____ practice tends to be seen as a creative industry, which includes advertising, distribution and selling.

   a. Marketing
   b. Product naming
   c. Customer acquisition management
   d. Marketing myopia

3. The _____ claims to be the world's largest retail trade association. Its members include department store, specialty, discount, catalog, Internet, and independent retailers, and chain restaurants and grocery stores. Members also include businesses that provide goods and services to retailers.
   a. National Retail Federation
   b. 180SearchAssistant
   c. Power III
   d. 6-3-5 Brainwriting

4. _____ is a standard point of view or personal prejudice. especially when the tendency interferes with the ability to be impartial, unprejudiced, or objective. The term _____ed is used to describe an action, judgment, or other outcome influenced by a prejudged perspective.
   a. Power III
   b. 180SearchAssistant
   c. 6-3-5 Brainwriting
   d. Bias

5. _____s are errors in measurement that lead to measured values being inconsistent when repeated measures of a constant attribute or quantity are taken. The word random indicates that they are inherently unpredictable, and have null expected value, namely, they are scattered about the true value, and tend to have null arithmetic mean when a measurement is repeated several times with the same instrument. All measurements are prone to _____.
   a. 180SearchAssistant
   b. Power III
   c. Systematic error
   d. Random error

6. _____ is that part of statistical practice concerned with the selection of individual observations intended to yield some knowledge about a population of concern, especially for the purposes of statistical inference. Each observation measures one or more properties (weight, location, etc.) of an observable entity enumerated to distinguish objects or individuals.
   a. Sports Marketing Group
   b. AStore
   c. Richard Buckminster 'Bucky' Fuller
   d. Sampling

7. In statistics, _____ or estimation error is the error caused by observing a sample instead of the whole population.

An estimate of a quantity of interest, such as an average or percentage, will generally be subject to sample-to-sample variation. These variations in the possible sample values of a statistic can theoretically be expressed as _____s, although in practice the exact _____ is typically unknown.

   a. Varimax rotation
   b. Two-tailed test
   c. Power III
   d. Sampling error

8. _____s are biases in measurement which lead to the situation where the mean of many separate measurements differs significantly from the actual value of the measured attribute. All measurements are prone to _____s, often of several different types. Sources of _____ may be imperfect calibration of measurement instruments, changes in the environment which interfere with the measurement process and sometimes imperfect methods of observation can be either zero error or percentage error.
   a. 180SearchAssistant
   b. Systematic bias
   c. Systematic error
   d. Power III

Chapter 5. Survey Research: The Profound Impact of the Internet

9. _____ a research method involving the use of questionnaires and/or statistical surveys to gather data about people and their thoughts and behaviours.
   a. Survey research
   b. Control chart
   c. Z-test
   d. T-test

10. _____ is the difference between a measured value of quantity and its true value. In statistics, an error is not a 'mistake'. Variability is an inherent part of things being measured and of the measurement process.
   a. ACNielsen
   b. ADTECH
   c. AMAX
   d. Observational error

11. A _____ is an error that occurs when a person performs an action on an object that is not the object intended. This error can be very disorienting and usually causes a brief loss of situation awareness or automation surprise if noticed right away. But much worse, if it goes unnoticed, it could cause more serious problems.
   a. 180SearchAssistant
   b. Motivation
   c. Description error
   d. Power III

12. A _____ is an explicit set of requirements to be satisfied by a material, product, or service.

In engineering, manufacturing, and business, it is vital for suppliers, purchasers, and users of materials, products, or services to understand and agree upon all requirements. A _____ is a type of a standard which is often referenced by a contract or procurement document.

   a. Specification
   b. New product development
   c. Product optimization
   d. Product development

13. A _____ is a research instrument consisting of a series of questions and other prompts for the purpose of gathering information from respondents. Although they are often designed for statistical analysis of the responses, this is not always the case. The _____ was invented by Sir Francis Galton.

a. Market research
b. Mystery shopping
c. Mystery shoppers
d. Questionnaire

14. _____ is a sales technique in which a salesperson walks from one door of a house to another trying to sell a product or service to the general public. A variant of this involves cold calling first, when another sales representative attempts to gain agreement that a salesperson should visit. _____ selling is usually conducted in the afternoon hours, when the majority of people are at home.
   a. Fast moving consumer goods
   b. Marketing management
   c. Performance-based advertising
   d. Door-to-door

15. _____ are used to collect quantitative information about items in a population. Surveys of human populations and institutions are common in political polling and government, health, social science and marketing research. A survey may focus on opinions or factual information depending on its purpose, and many surveys involve administering questions to individuals.
   a. Gross Margin Return on Inventory Investment
   b. BeyondROI
   c. Convergent
   d. Statistical surveys

16. Procter is a surname, and may also refer to:

   - Bryan Waller Procter (pseud. Barry Cornwall), English poet
   - Goodwin Procter, American law firm
   - _____, consumer products multinational

   a. Black PRies
   b. Convergent
   c. Procter ' Gamble
   d. Flyer

17. _____ is a telephone surveying technique in which the interviewer follows a script provided by a software application. The software is able to customize the flow of the questionnaire based on the answers provided, as well as information already known about the participant.

CATI may function in the following manner

- A computerized questionnaire is administered to respondents over the telephone.
- The interviewer sits in front of a computer screen
- Upon command, the computer dials the telephone number to be called.
- When contact is made, the interviewer reads the questions posed on the computer screen and records the respondent's answers directly into the computer.
- Interim and update reports can be compiled instantaneously, as the data are being collected.
- CATI software has built-in logic, which also enhances data accuracy.
- The program will personalize questions and control for logically incorrect answers, such as percentage answers that do not add up to 100 percent.
- The software has built-in branching logic, which will skip questions that are not applicable or will probe for more detail when warranted.

a. 180SearchAssistant
b. 6-3-5 Brainwriting
c. Power III
d. Computer-assisted telephone interviewing

18. A longitudinal study is a correlational research study that involves repeated observations of the same items over long periods of time -- often many decades. It is a type of observational study. _____ are often used in psychology to study developmental trends across the life span.
a. Study design
b. Power III
c. Longitudinal studies
d. 180SearchAssistant

19. _____ is an American marketing research and consulting firm based in Arlington, Texas. It also operates the American Consumer Opinion online panel, which is made up of over seven million people. .
a. Chief executive officer
b. Power III
c. Financial analyst
d. Decision Analyst

20. Consumer market research is a form of applied sociology that concentrates on understanding the behaviours, whims and preferences, of consumers in a market-based economy, and aims to understand the effects and comparative success of marketing campaigns. The field of consumer _____ as a statistical science was pioneered by Arthur Nielsen with the founding of the ACNielsen Company in 1923.

Thus _____ is the systematic and objective identification, collection, analysis, and dissemination of information for the purpose of assisting management in decision making related to the identification and solution of problems and opportunities in marketing.

a. Marketing research process
b. Marketing research
c. Logit analysis
d. Focus group

21. _____ is the practice of promoting products and services using digital distribution channels to reach consumers in a timely, relevant, personal and cost-effective manner.

Whilst _____ does include many of the techniques and practices contained within the category of Internet Marketing, it extends beyond this by including other channels with which to reach people that do not require the use of The Internet. As a result of this non-reliance on the Internet, the field of _____ includes a whole host of elements such as mobile phones, sms/mms, display / banner ads and digital outdoor.

a. Global marketing
b. Relationship marketing
c. Diversity marketing
d. Digital Marketing

22. _____ and its predecessor, Secure Sockets Layer (SSL), are cryptographic protocols that provide security and data integrity for communications over TCP/IP networks such as the Internet. _____ and SSL encrypt the segments of network connections at the Transport Layer end-to-end.

Several versions of the protocols are in wide-spread use in applications like web browsing, electronic mail, Internet faxing, instant messaging and voice-over-IP (VoIP.)

a. Power III
b. 180SearchAssistant
c. HyperText Transfer Protocol
d. Transport Layer Security

23. _____ is an advertisement in which a particular product specifically mentions a competitor by name for the express purpose of showing why the competitor is inferior to the product naming it.

This should not be confused with parody advertisements, where a fictional product is being advertised for the purpose of poking fun at the particular advertisement, nor should it be confused with the use of a coined brand name for the purpose of comparing the product without actually naming an actual competitor. ('Wikipedia tastes better and is less filling than the Encyclopedia Galactica.')

In the 1980s, during what has been referred to as the cola wars, soft-drink manufacturer Pepsi ran a series of advertisements where people, caught on hidden camera, in a blind taste test, chose Pepsi over rival Coca-Cola.

   a. Cost per conversion
   b. Heavy-up
   c. Comparative advertising
   d. GL-70

24. _____ refer to a collection of facts usually collected as the result of experience, observation or experiment or a set of premises. This may consist of numbers, words particularly as measurements or observations of a set of variables. _____ are often viewed as a lowest level of abstraction from which information and knowledge are derived.

   a. Pearson product-moment correlation coefficient
   b. Data
   c. Sample size
   d. Mean

25. _____ is either an activity of a living being (such as a human), consisting of receiving knowledge of the outside world through the senses, or the recording of data using scientific instruments. The term may also refer to any datum collected during this activity.

The scientific method requires _____s of nature to formulate and test hypotheses.

   a. ADTECH
   b. AMAX
   c. Observation
   d. ACNielsen

26. In economics, _____ is the desire to own something and the ability to pay for it. The term _____ signifies the ability or the willingness to buy a particular commodity at a given point of time .

a. Market dominance
b. Discretionary spending
c. Market system
d. Demand

27. _____ is a computer program used for statistical analysis.

_____ (originally, Statistical Package for the Social Sciences) was released in its first version in 1968 after being founded by Norman Nie and C. Hadlai Hull. Nie was then a political science postgraduate at Stanford University,and now Research Professor in the Department of Political Science at Stanford and Professor Emeritus of Political Science at the University of Chicago.

a. 6-3-5 Brainwriting
b. SPSS
c. Power III
d. 180SearchAssistant

28. The _____ is the number of new cases per unit of person-time at risk. In the same example as above, the _____ is 14 cases per 1000 person-years, because the incidence proportion (28 per 1,000) is divided by the number of years (two.) Using person-time rather than just time handles situations where the amount of observation time differs between people, or when the population at risk varies with time.

a. ADTECH
b. ACNielsen
c. AMAX
d. Incidence rate

29. A _____ is a structured collection of records or data that is stored in a computer system. The structure is achieved by organizing the data according to a _____ model. The model in most common use today is the relational model.

a. 6-3-5 Brainwriting
b. Database
c. 180SearchAssistant
d. Power III

30. _____ is a broad label that refers to any individuals or households that use goods and services generated within the economy. The concept of a _____ is used in different contexts, so that the usage and significance of the term may vary.

A _____ is a person who uses any product or service.

a. 6-3-5 Brainwriting
b. Power III
c. 180SearchAssistant
d. Consumer

31. _____ is a specialized form of marketing research conducted to improve the efficiency of advertising. According to MarketConscious.com, 'It may focus on a specific ad or campaign, or may be directed at a more general understanding of how advertising works or how consumers use the information in advertising. It can entail a variety of research approaches, including psychological, sociological, economic, and other perspectives.'

1879 - N.W. Ayer conducts custom research in an attempt to win the advertising business of Nichols-Shepard Co., a manufacturer of agricultural machinery.

a. Advertising Research
b. INVISTA
c. Electrolux
d. American Medical Association

32. The _____ is a nonprofit industry association for creating, aggregating, synthesizing and sharing the knowledge in the fields of advertising and media. It was founded in 1936 by the Association of National Advertisers and the American Association of Advertising Agencies. Its stated mission is to improve the practice of advertising, marketing and media research in pursuit of more effective marketing and advertising communications.

a. IDDEA
b. Advertising Research Foundation
c. ACNielsen
d. Intent scale translation

33. _____ refers to the evolving trend in marketing whereby marketing has moved from a transaction-based effort to a conversation. The definition of _____ comes from John Deighton at Harvard, who says _____ is the ability to address the customer, remember what the customer says and address the customer again in a way that illustrates that we remember what the customer has told us (Deighton 1996.) _____ is not synonymous with online marketing, although _____ processes are facilitated by internet technology.

a. InfoNU
b. European Information Technology Observatory
c. Outsourcing relationship management
d. Interactive Marketing

34. _____, fundamental research (sometimes pure research), is research carried out to increase understanding of fundamental principles. Many times the end results have no direct or immediate commercial benefits, which is to say that _____ can be thought of as arising out of pure curiosity. However, in the long term it is the basis for many commercial products and applied research.
   a. Reference value
   b. Response rate
   c. Power III
   d. Basic research

Chapter 6. Primary Data Collection: Observation

1. Procter is a surname, and may also refer to:

   - Bryan Waller Procter (pseud. Barry Cornwall), English poet
   - Goodwin Procter, American law firm
   - _____, consumer products multinational

   a. Convergent
   b. Flyer
   c. Black PRies
   d. Procter ' Gamble

2. _____ is a global marketing research firm, with worldwide headquarters in New York City. Regional headquarters for North America are located in Schaumburg, IL. As of 2008, its the part of The Nielsen Company.
   a. E-Detailing
   b. Alloy Entertainment
   c. InfoNU
   d. ACNielsen

3. _____ is either an activity of a living being (such as a human), consisting of receiving knowledge of the outside world through the senses, or the recording of data using scientific instruments. The term may also refer to any datum collected during this activity.

   The scientific method requires _____s of nature to formulate and test hypotheses.

   a. ADTECH
   b. AMAX
   c. Observation
   d. ACNielsen

4. Mystery shopping or Mystery Consumer is a tool used by market research companies to measure quality of retail service or gather specific information about products and services. _____ posing as normal customers perform specific tasks-- such as purchasing a product, asking questions, registering complaints or behaving in a certain way - and then provide detailed reports or feedback about their experiences.

   Mystery shopping began in the 1940s as a way to measure employee integrity.

a. Market research
b. Questionnaire
c. Mystery shopping
d. Mystery shoppers

5. _____ or Mystery Consumer is a tool used by market research companies to measure quality of retail service or gather specific information about products and services. Mystery shoppers posing as normal customers perform specific tasks-- such as purchasing a product, asking questions, registering complaints or behaving in a certain way - and then provide detailed reports or feedback about their experiences.

_____ began in the 1940s as a way to measure employee integrity.

a. Questionnaire
b. Market research
c. Mystery shoppers
d. Mystery shopping

6. _____ is the examining of goods or services from retailers with the intent to purchase at that time. _____ is an activity of selection and/or purchase. In some contexts it is considered a leisure activity as well as an economic one.
a. Discount store
b. Khodebshchik
c. Hawkers
d. Shopping

7. The general definition of an _____ is an evaluation of a person, organization, system, process, project or product. _____s are performed to ascertain the validity and reliability of information; also to provide an assessment of a system's internal control. The goal of an _____ is to express an opinion on the person/organization/system (etc) in question, under evaluation based on work done on a test basis.
a. AMAX
b. Audit
c. ADTECH
d. ACNielsen

8. Human beings are also considered to be _____ because they have the ability to change raw materials into valuable _____. The term Human _____ can also be defined as the skills, energies, talents, abilities and knowledge that are used for the production of goods or the rendering of services. While taking into account human beings as _____, the following things have to be kept in mind:

- The size of the population
- The capabilities of the individuals in that population

Many _____ cannot be consumed in their original form. They have to be processed in order to change them into more usable commodities.

a. Power III
b. 180SearchAssistant
c. 6-3-5 Brainwriting
d. Resources

9. A _____ is a form of qualitative research in which a group of people are asked about their attitude towards a product, service, concept, advertisement, idea, or packaging. Questions are asked in an interactive group setting where participants are free to talk with other group members.

Ernest Dichter originated the idea of having a 'group therapy' for products and this process is what became known as a _____.

a. Logit analysis
b. Marketing research process
c. Focus group
d. Cross tabulation

10. _____ psychogalvanic reflex is a method of measuring the electrical resistance of the skin. There has been a long history of electrodermal activity research, most of it dealing with spontaneous fluctuations. Most investigators accept the phenomenon without understanding exactly what it means.

a. Galvanic skin response
b. Power III
c. 6-3-5 Brainwriting
d. 180SearchAssistant

11. _____ refer to a collection of facts usually collected as the result of experience, observation or experiment or a set of premises. This may consist of numbers, words particularly as measurements or observations of a set of variables. _____ are often viewed as a lowest level of abstraction from which information and knowledge are derived.

a. Data
b. Mean
c. Pearson product-moment correlation coefficient
d. Sample size

12. _____ is the process of measuring either the point of gaze ('where we are looking') or the motion of an eye relative to the head. An eye tracker is a device for measuring eye positions and eye movements. Eye trackers are used in research on the visual system, in psychology, in cognitive linguistics and in product design.

a. ACNielsen
b. AMAX
c. ADTECH
d. Eye tracking

13. In psychology, philosophy, and the cognitive sciences, _____ is the process of attaining awareness or understanding of sensory information. It is a task far more complex than was imagined in the 1950s and 1960s, when it was predicted that building perceiving machines would take about a decade, a goal which is still very far from fruition. The word _____ comes from the Latin words _____, percepio, meaning 'receiving, collecting, action of taking possession, apprehension with the mind or senses.'

_____ is one of the oldest fields in psychology.

a. 180SearchAssistant
b. Groupthink
c. Power III
d. Perception

14. _____ is an advertisement in which a particular product specifically mentions a competitor by name for the express purpose of showing why the competitor is inferior to the product naming it.

This should not be confused with parody advertisements, where a fictional product is being advertised for the purpose of poking fun at the particular advertisement, nor should it be confused with the use of a coined brand name for the purpose of comparing the product without actually naming an actual competitor. ('Wikipedia tastes better and is less filling than the Encyclopedia Galactica.')

In the 1980s, during what has been referred to as the cola wars, soft-drink manufacturer Pepsi ran a series of advertisements where people, caught on hidden camera, in a blind taste test, chose Pepsi over rival Coca-Cola.

a. GL-70
b. Cost per conversion
c. Heavy-up
d. Comparative advertising

15. _____ is a form of communication that typically attempts to persuade potential customers to purchase or to consume more of a particular brand of product or service. 'While now central to the contemporary global economy and the reproduction of global production networks, it is only quite recently that _____ has been more than a marginal influence on patterns of sales and production. The formation of modern _____ was intimately bound up with the emergence of new forms of monopoly capitalism around the end of the 19th and beginning of the 20th century as one element in corporate strategies to create, organize and where possible control markets, especially for mass produced consumer goods.
   a. ACNielsen
   b. ADTECH
   c. Advertising
   d. AMAX

16. _____ is a radio audience research company in the United States which collects listener data on radio audiences similar to that collected by Nielsen Media Research on television audiences. It was founded as American Research Bureau by Jim Seiler in 1949 and became bi-coastal by merging with L.A. based Coffin, Cooper and Clay in the early 1950s. ARB's initial business was the collection of television broadcast ratings exclusively.
   a. Access Commerce
   b. American Cancer Society
   c. American Heart Association
   d. Arbitron

17. The _____ is a global navigation satellite system (GNSS) developed by the United States Department of Defense and managed by the United States Air Force 50th Space Wing. It is the only fully functional GNSS in the world, can be used freely, and is often used by civilians for navigation purposes. It uses a constellation of between 24 and 32 Medium Earth Orbit satellites that transmit precise microwave signals, which allow _____ receivers to determine their current location, the time, and their velocity.
   a. Power III
   b. 6-3-5 Brainwriting
   c. Global positioning system
   d. 180SearchAssistant

18. The _____ is the lead trade association representing the outdoor advertising industry. Founded in 1891, the OAAA is dedicated to promoting, protecting and advancing outdoor advertising and out-of-home advertising interests in the U.S. With nearly 1,100 member companies, the OAAA represents more than 90 percent of industry revenues.

Outdoor formats fall into one of four major categories: Billboards

Street furniture

Transit

Alternative

The large American outdoor poster (more than 50 square feet) originated in New York in Jared Bell's office where he printed posters for the circus in 1835.

a. American Lung Association
b. Arbitron
c. American Cancer Society
d. Outdoor Advertising Association of America

19. A _____ is a tool used to measure the viewing habits of TV and cable audiences.

The _____ is a 'box', about the size of a paperback book. The box is hooked up to each television set and is accompanied by a remote control unit.

a. 6-3-5 Brainwriting
b. Power III
c. 180SearchAssistant
d. People meter

20. In marketing, _____ has come to mean the process by which marketers try to create an image or identity in the minds of their target market for its product, brand, or organization. It is the 'relative competitive comparison' their product occupies in a given market as perceived by the target market.

Re-_____ involves changing the identity of a product, relative to the identity of competing products, in the collective minds of the target market.

a. Positioning
b. GE matrix
c. Containerization
d. Moratorium

21. A _____ is an optical machine-readable representation of data. Originally, _____s represented data in the widths (lines) and the spacings of parallel lines and may be referred to as linear or 1D (1 dimensional) barcodes or symbologies. But they also come in patterns of squares, dots, hexagons and other geometric patterns within images termed 2D (2 dimensional) matrix codes or symbologies.
a. 6-3-5 Brainwriting
b. Power III
c. Bar code
d. 180SearchAssistant

22. _____ is defined by the American _____ Association as the activity, set of institutions, and processes for creating, communicating, delivering, and exchanging offerings that have value for customers, clients, partners, and society at large. The term developed from the original meaning which referred literally to going to market, as in shopping, or going to a market to sell goods or services.

_____ practice tends to be seen as a creative industry, which includes advertising, distribution and selling.

a. Marketing myopia
b. Customer acquisition management
c. Product naming
d. Marketing

23. Consumer market research is a form of applied sociology that concentrates on understanding the behaviours, whims and preferences, of consumers in a market-based economy, and aims to understand the effects and comparative success of marketing campaigns. The field of consumer _____ as a statistical science was pioneered by Arthur Nielsen with the founding of the ACNielsen Company in 1923 .

Thus _____ is the systematic and objective identification, collection, analysis, and dissemination of information for the purpose of assisting management in decision making related to the identification and solution of problems and opportunities in marketing.

a. Marketing research process
b. Focus group
c. Logit analysis
d. Marketing research

24. A _____ is a statement or claim that a particular event will occur in the future in more certain terms than a forecast. The etymology of this word is Latin . In regards to predicting the future Howard H. Stevenson Says, '_____ is at least two things: Important and hard.' Important, because we have to act, and hard because we have to realize the future we want, and what is the best way to get there.

a. Prediction
b. Power III
c. 6-3-5 Brainwriting
d. 180SearchAssistant

25. _____ is the process of gathering and analysing information regarding customers; their details and their activities, in order to build deeper and more effective customer relationships and improve strategic decision making.

Consumer Intelligence is also the name of a leading company within the UK Research industry that is referenced in large number of Advertising campaigns by companies such as Asda, Budget Compare The Market, Churchill, Direct Line, MoneySupermarket, Norwich Union and many others.

_____ is a key component of effective Customer Relationship Management, and when effectively implemented it is a rich source of insight into the behaviour and experience of a company's customer base.

a. Pop-up ads
b. Project Portfolio Management
c. Power III
d. Customer intelligence

26. _____ is the generic term for a class of software music sequencers which, in their purest form, allow the user to arrange sound samples stepwise on a timeline across several monophonic channels. A _____'s interface is primarily numeric; notes are entered via the alphanumeric keys of the computer keyboard, while parameters, effects and so forth are entered in hexadecimal. A complete song consists of several small multi-channel patterns chained together via a master list.
a. 180SearchAssistant
b. Power III
c. 6-3-5 Brainwriting
d. Tracker

Chapter 7. Primary Data Collection: Experimentation

1. _____, fundamental research (sometimes pure research), is research carried out to increase understanding of fundamental principles. Many times the end results have no direct or immediate commercial benefits, which is to say that _____ can be thought of as arising out of pure curiosity. However, in the long term it is the basis for many commercial products and applied research.

   a. Basic research
   b. Response rate
   c. Power III
   d. Reference value

2. A _____ applies the scientific method to experimentally examine an intervention in the real world (or as many experimental economists like to say, naturally-occurring environments) rather than in the laboratory. _____s, like lab experiments, generally randomize subjects (or other sampling units) into treatment and control groups and compare outcomes between these groups. Clinical trials of pharmaceuticals are one example of _____s.

   a. 180SearchAssistant
   b. Power III
   c. Response variable
   d. Field experiment

3. _____ is the validity of (causal) inferences in scientific studies, usually based on experiments as experimental validity.

   Inferences are said to possess _____ if a causal relation between two variables is properly demonstrated. A causal inference may be based on a relation when three criteria are satisfied:

   1. the 'cause' precedes the 'effect' in time (temporal precedence),
   2. the 'cause' and the 'effect' are related (covariation), and
   3. there are no plausible alternative explanations for the observed covariation (nonspuriousness).

   In scientific experimental settings, researchers often manipulate a variable (the independent variable) to see what effect it has on a second variable (the dependent variable) For example, a researcher might, for different experimental groups, manipulate the dosage of a particular drug between groups to see what effect it has on health. In this example, the researcher wants to make a causal inference, namely, that different doses of the drug may be held responsible for observed changes or differences.

   a. AMAX
   b. ACNielsen
   c. ADTECH
   d. Internal validity

Chapter 7. Primary Data Collection: Experimentation

4. In economics, an externality or spillover of an economic transaction is an impact on a party that is not directly involved in the transaction. In such a case, prices do not reflect the full costs or benefits in production or consumption of a product or service. A positive impact is called an _____ benefit, while a negative impact is called an _____ cost.

   a. External
   b. ACNielsen
   c. AMAX
   d. ADTECH

5. _____ is the validity of generalized (causal) inferences in scientific studies, usually based on experiments as experimental validity.

Inferences about cause-effect relationships based on a specific scientific study are said to possess _____ if they may be generalized from the unique and idiosyncratic settings, procedures and participants to other populations and conditions Causal inferences said to possess high degrees of _____ can reasonably be expected to apply (a) to the target population of the study (i.e. from which the sample was drawn) (also referred to as population validity), and (b) to the universe of other populations (e.g. across time and space.)

The most common loss of _____ comes from the fact that experiments using human participants often employ small samples obtained from a single geographic location or with idiosyncratic features (e.g. volunteers.)

   a. AMAX
   b. ACNielsen
   c. ADTECH
   d. External Validity

6. _____ are variables other than the independent variable that may bear any effect on the behavior of the subject being studied.

   _____ are often classified into three main types:

   1. Subject variables, which are the characteristics of the individuals being studied that might affect their actions. These variables include age, gender, health status, mood, background, etc.
   2. Experimental variables are characteristics of the persons conducting the experiment which might influence how a person behaves. Gender, the presence of racial discrimination, language, or other factors may qualify as such variables.
   3. Situational variables are features of the environment in which the study or research was conducted, which have a bearing on the outcome of the experiment in a negative way. Included are the air temperature, level of activity, lighting, and the time of day.

There are two strategies of controlling _____. Either a potentially influential variable is kept the same for all subjects in the research, or they balance the variables in a group.

Chapter 7. Primary Data Collection: Experimentation

Take for example an experiment, in which a salesperson sells clothing on a door-to-door basis.

a. ADTECH
b. AMAX
c. ACNielsen
d. Extraneous variables

7. _____s are used in open sentences. For instance, in the formula x + 1 = 5, x is a _____ which represents an 'unknown' number. _____s are often represented by letters of the Roman alphabet, or those of other alphabets, such as Greek, and use other special symbols.

a. Quantitative
b. Book of business
c. Personalization
d. Variable

8. _____ is a distortion of evidence or data that arises from the way that the data are collected. It is sometimes referred to as the selection effect. The term _____ most often refers to the distortion of a statistical analysis, due to the method of collecting samples.

a. Selection bias
b. Power III
c. 180SearchAssistant
d. Systematic sampling

9. _____ is a standard point of view or personal prejudice. especially when the tendency interferes with the ability to be impartial, unprejudiced, or objective. The term _____ed is used to describe an action, judgment, or other outcome influenced by a prejudged perspective.

a. 180SearchAssistant
b. Bias
c. Power III
d. 6-3-5 Brainwriting

10. _____ is that part of statistical practice concerned with the selection of individual observations intended to yield some knowledge about a population of concern, especially for the purposes of statistical inference. Each observation measures one or more properties (weight, location, etc.) of an observable entity enumerated to distinguish objects or individuals.

a. Richard Buckminster 'Bucky' Fuller
b. Sampling
c. Sports Marketing Group
d. AStore

11. In statistics, _____ has two related meanings:

- the arithmetic _____
- the expected value of a random variable, which is also called the population _____.

It is sometimes stated that the '_____' _____ s average. This is incorrect if '_____' is taken in the specific sense of 'arithmetic _____' as there are different types of averages: the _____, median, and mode. For instance, average house prices almost always use the median value for the average. These three types of averages are all measures of locations.

a. Heteroskedastic
b. Confidence interval
c. Standard normal distribution
d. Mean

12. In economics, business, retail, and accounting, a _____ is the value of money that has been used up to produce something, and hence is not available for use anymore. In economics, a _____ is an alternative that is given up as a result of a decision. In business, the _____ may be one of acquisition, in which case the amount of money expended to acquire it is counted as _____.

a. Transaction cost
b. Variable cost
c. Cost
d. Fixed costs

13. _____ is the process whereby companies use cost accounting to report or control the various costs of doing business.

The term _____ is widely used in business today. Unfortunately _____ has no uniform definition.

a. Customer profitability
b. Cost management
c. Power III
d. 180SearchAssistant

Chapter 7. Primary Data Collection: Experimentation

14. The terms '_____' and 'independent variable' are used in similar but subtly different ways in mathematics and statistics as part of the standard terminology in those subjects. They are used to distinguish between two types of quantities being considered, separating them into those available at the start of a process and those being created by it, where the latter (_____s) are dependent on the former (independent variables.)

In traditional calculus, a function is defined as a relation between two terms called variables because their values vary.

   a. Power III
   b. Dependent variable
   c. 180SearchAssistant
   d. Field experiment

15. _____ is the presence of a minor constituent in another chemical or mixture, often at the trace level. In chemistry, the term usually describes a single chemical, but in specialized fields the term can also mean chemical mixtures, even up to the level of cellular materials.

All chemicals contain some level of _____.

   a. 180SearchAssistant
   b. 6-3-5 Brainwriting
   c. Power III
   d. Contamination

16. _____ is the realization of an application idea, model, design, specification, standard, algorithm an _____ is a realization of a technical specification or algorithm as a program, software component, or other computer system. Many _____s may exist for a given specification or standard.
   a. Implementation
   b. ADTECH
   c. AMAX
   d. ACNielsen

Chapter 7. Primary Data Collection: Experimentation

17. A number of different _____s are indicated below.

- Randomized controlled trial
    - Double-blind randomized trial
    - Single-blind randomized trial
    - Non-blind trial
- Nonrandomized trial (quasi-experiment)
    - Interrupted time series design (measures on a sample or a series of samples from the same population are obtained several times before and after a manipulated event or a naturally occurring event) - considered a type of quasi-experiment

- Cohort study
    - Prospective cohort
    - Retrospective cohort
    - Time series study
- Case-control study
    - Nested case-control study
- Cross-sectional study
    - Community survey (a type of cross-sectional study)

When choosing a _____, many factors must be taken into account. Different types of studies are subject to different types of bias. For example, recall bias is likely to occur in cross-sectional or case-control studies where subjects are asked to recall exposure to risk factors.

a. Power III
b. Longitudinal studies
c. 180SearchAssistant
d. Study design

18. A _____, in the field of business and marketing, is a geographic region or demographic group used to gauge the viability of a product or service in the mass market prior to a wide scale roll-out. The criteria used to judge the acceptability of a _____ region or group include:

1. a population that is demographically similar to the proposed target market; and
2. relative isolation from densely populated media markets so that advertising to the test audience can be efficient and economical.

The _____ ideally aims to duplicate 'everything' - promotion and distribution as well as `product' - on a smaller scale. The technique replicates, typically in one area, what is planned to occur in a national launch; and the results are very carefully monitored, so that they can be extrapolated to projected national results. The `area' may be any one of the following:

- Television area
- Test town
- Residential neighborhood
- Test site

A number of decisions have to be taken about any _____:

- Which _____?
- What is to be tested?
- How long a test?
- What are the success criteria?

The simple go or no-go decision, together with the related reduction of risk, is normally the main justification for the expense of _____s. At the same time, however, such _____s can be used to test specific elements of a new product's marketing mix; possibly the version of the product itself, the promotional message and media spend, the distribution channels and the price.

a. 180SearchAssistant
b. Test market
c. Preadolescence
d. Power III

19. _____ is defined by the American _____ Association as the activity, set of institutions, and processes for creating, communicating, delivering, and exchanging offerings that have value for customers, clients, partners, and society at large. The term developed from the original meaning which referred literally to going to market, as in shopping, or going to a market to sell goods or services.

_____ practice tends to be seen as a creative industry, which includes advertising, distribution and selling.

a. Marketing
b. Product naming
c. Customer acquisition management
d. Marketing myopia

Chapter 7. Primary Data Collection: Experimentation 53

20. Procter is a surname, and may also refer to:

   - Bryan Waller Procter (pseud. Barry Cornwall), English poet
   - Goodwin Procter, American law firm
   - _____, consumer products multinational

   a. Convergent
   b. Black PRies
   c. Flyer
   d. Procter ' Gamble

21. _____ is the imitation of some real thing, state of affairs, or process. The act of simulating something generally entails representing certain key characteristics or behaviors of a selected physical or abstract system.

   _____ is used in many contexts, including the modeling of natural systems or human systems in order to gain insight into their functioning.

   a. 180SearchAssistant
   b. Power III
   c. 6-3-5 Brainwriting
   d. Simulation

Chapter 8. The Concept of Measurement

1. The '_____' is an expression which typically refers to the theory of scale types developed by the Harvard psychologist Stanley Smith Stevens In this article Stevens claimed that all measurement in science was conducted using four different types of numerical scales which he called 'nominal', 'ordinal', 'interval' and 'ratio'.
   a. 6-3-5 Brainwriting
   b. Levels of measurement
   c. Power III
   d. 180SearchAssistant

2. In probability theory and statistics, _____ indicates the strength and direction of a linear relationship between two random variables. That is in contrast with the usage of the term in colloquial speech, denoting any relationship, not necessarily linear. In general statistical usage, _____ or co-relation refers to the departure of two random variables from independence.
   a. Frequency distribution
   b. Correlation
   c. Mean
   d. Probability

3. _____ and formal equivalence are two approaches to translation. The dynamic (also known as functional equivalence) attempts to convey the thought expressed in a source text (if necessary, at the expense of literalness, original word order, the source text's grammatical voice, etc.), while formal attempts to render the text word-for-word (if necessary, at the expense of natural expression in the target language.) The two approaches represent emphasis, respectively, on readability and on literal fidelity to the source text.
   a. 180SearchAssistant
   b. 6-3-5 Brainwriting
   c. Power III
   d. Dynamic equivalence

4. The Oxford University Press defines _____ as 'marketing on a worldwide scale reconciling or taking commercial advantage of global operational differences, similarities and opportunities in order to meet global objectives.' Oxford University Press' Glossary of Marketing Terms.

Here are three reasons for the shift from domestic to _____ as given by the authors of the textbook, _____ Management--3rd Edition by Masaaki Kotabe and Kristiaan Helsen, 2004.

One of the product categories in which global competition has been easy to track is in U.S. automotive sales.

Chapter 8. The Concept of Measurement

a. Guerrilla Marketing
b. Global marketing
c. Digital marketing
d. Diversity marketing

5. _____ is defined by the American _____ Association as the activity, set of institutions, and processes for creating, communicating, delivering, and exchanging offerings that have value for customers, clients, partners, and society at large. The term developed from the original meaning which referred literally to going to market, as in shopping, or going to a market to sell goods or services.

_____ practice tends to be seen as a creative industry, which includes advertising, distribution and selling.

a. Product naming
b. Marketing
c. Customer acquisition management
d. Marketing myopia

6. Consumer market research is a form of applied sociology that concentrates on understanding the behaviours, whims and preferences, of consumers in a market-based economy, and aims to understand the effects and comparative success of marketing campaigns. The field of consumer _____ as a statistical science was pioneered by Arthur Nielsen with the founding of the ACNielsen Company in 1923.

Thus _____ is the systematic and objective identification, collection, analysis, and dissemination of information for the purpose of assisting management in decision making related to the identification and solution of problems and opportunities in marketing.

a. Focus group
b. Logit analysis
c. Marketing research process
d. Marketing research

7. _____ is either an activity of a living being (such as a human), consisting of receiving knowledge of the outside world through the senses, or the recording of data using scientific instruments. The term may also refer to any datum collected during this activity.

The scientific method requires _____s of nature to formulate and test hypotheses.

a. AMAX
b. ACNielsen
c. ADTECH
d. Observation

8. _____ a research method involving the use of questionnaires and/or statistical surveys to gather data about people and their thoughts and behaviours.
   a. Control chart
   b. Z-test
   c. T-test
   d. Survey research

9. _____ is a statistical method used to examine how reliable a test is: A test is performed twice, e.g., the same test is given to a group of subjects at two different times. Each subject should score different than the other subjects, but if the test is reliable then each subject should score the same in both test.

Valentin Rousson, Theo Gasser, and Burkhardt Seifert, (2002) 'Assessing intrarater, interrater and _____ reliability of continuous measurements,' Statistics in Medicine 21:3431-3446.

   a. 6-3-5 Brainwriting
   b. 180SearchAssistant
   c. Test-retest
   d. Power III

10. In statistics and research, _____ is a measure based on the correlations between different items on the same test (or the same subscale on a larger test.) It measures whether several items that propose to measure the same general construct produce similar scores. For example, if a respondent expressed agreement with the statements 'I like to ride bicycles' and 'I've enjoyed riding bicycles in the past', and disagreement with the statement 'I hate bicycles', this would be indicative of good _____ of the test.
   a. ACNielsen
   b. ADTECH
   c. Internal consistency
   d. AMAX

Chapter 8. The Concept of Measurement

11. In social science and psychometrics, _____ refers to whether a scale measures or correlates with a theorized psychological construct (such as 'fluid intelligence'.) It is related to the theoretical ideas behind the personality trait under consideration; a non-existent concept in the physical sense may be suggested as a method of organising how personality can be viewed. The unobservable idea of a unidimensional easier-to-harder dimension must be 'constructed' in the words of human language and graphics.
    a. Construct validity
    b. Criterion validity
    c. Discriminant validity
    d. Predictive validity

12. In psychometrics, _____ refers to the extent to which a measure represents all facets of a given social construct. For example, a depression scale may lack _____ if it only assesses the affective dimension of depression but fails to take into account the behavioral dimension. An element of subjectivity exists in relation to determining _____, which requires a degree of agreement about what a particular personality trait such as extraversion represents.
    a. Convergent validity
    b. Criterion validity
    c. Predictive validity
    d. Content validity

13. _____ is a property of a test intended to measure something. The test is said to have _____ if it 'looks like' it is going to measure what it is supposed to measure. For instance, if you prepare a test to measure whether students can perform multiplication, and the people you show it to all agree that it looks like a good test of multiplication ability, you have shown the _____ of your test.
    a. Power III
    b. 180SearchAssistant
    c. Selective distortion
    d. Face validity

14. _____ is a parameter used in sociology, psychology, and other psychometric or behavioral sciences. _____ is demonstrated where a test correlates well with a measure that has previously been validated. The two measures may be for the same construct, or for different, but presumably related, constructs.
    a. Discriminant validity
    b. Criterion validity
    c. Construct validity
    d. Concurrent validity

15. A _____ is a statement or claim that a particular event will occur in the future in more certain terms than a forecast. The etymology of this word is Latin . In regards to predicting the future Howard H. Stevenson Says, ' _____ is at least two things: Important and hard.' Important, because we have to act, and hard because we have to realize the future we want, and what is the best way to get there.
   a. Prediction
   b. 6-3-5 Brainwriting
   c. Power III
   d. 180SearchAssistant

16. In psychometrics, _____ is the extent to which a score on a scale or test predicts scores on some criterion measure.

For example, the validity of a cognitive test for job performance is the correlation between test scores and, for example, supervisor performance ratings. Such a cognitive test would have _____ if the observed correlation were statistically significant.

   a. Criterion validity
   b. Discriminant validity
   c. Convergent validity
   d. Predictive validity

17. In the absence of a more specific context, convergence denotes the approach toward a definite value, as time goes on; or to a definite point, a common view or opinion, or toward a fixed or equilibrium state. _____ is the adjectival form, and also a noun meaning an iterative approximation.

In mathematics, convergence describes limiting behaviour, particularly of an infinite sequence or series, toward some limit.

   a. Strict liability
   b. Convergent
   c. Good things come to those who wait
   d. Geo

18. _____ is the degree to which an operation is similar to (converges on) other operations that it theoretically should also be similar to. For instance, to show the _____ of a test of mathematics skills, the scores on the test can be correlated with scores on other tests that are also designed to measure basic mathematics ability. High correlations between the test scores would be evidence of a _____.

a. Criterion validity
b. Content validity
c. Discriminant validity
d. Convergent validity

19. In algebra, the _____ of a polynomial with real or complex coefficients is a certain expression in the coefficients of the polynomial which is equal to zero if and only if the polynomial has a multiple root (i.e. a root with multiplicity greater than one) in the complex numbers. For example, the _____ of the quadratic polynomial

$$ax^2 + bx + c \text{ is } b^2 - 4ac.$$

The _____ of the cubic polynomial

$$ax^3 + bx^2 + cx + d \text{ is } b^2c^2 - 4ac^3 - 4b^3d - 27a^2d^2 + 18abcd.$$

a. Lifestyle center
b. Flighting
c. Consumption Map
d. Discriminant

20. _____ describes the degree to which the operationalization is not similar to (diverges from) other operationalizations that it theoretically should not be similar to.

Campbell and Fiske (1959) introduced the concept of _____ within their discussion on evaluating test validity. They stressed the importance of using both discriminant and convergent validation techniques when assessing new tests.

a. Convergent validity
b. Criterion validity
c. Predictive validity
d. Discriminant validity

21. A _____ is a psychometric scale commonly used in questionnaires, and is the most widely used scale in survey research. When responding to a Likert questionnaire item, respondents specify their level of agreement to a statement. The scale is named after its inventor, psychologist Rensis Likert.

Chapter 8. The Concept of Measurement

a. Power III
b. Semantic differential
c. Likert scale
d. Factor analysis

22. In grammar, the _____ is the form of an adjective or adverb which denotes the degree or grade by which a person, thing and is used in this context with a subordinating conjunction, such as than, as...as, etc.

The structure of a _____ in English consists normally of the positive form of the adjective or adverb, plus the suffix -er e.g. 'he is taller than his father is', or 'the village is less picturesque than the town nearby'.

a. 6-3-5 Brainwriting
b. 180SearchAssistant
c. Power III
d. Comparative

23. In statistics, _____ has two related meanings:

- the arithmetic _____
- the expected value of a random variable, which is also called the population _____.

It is sometimes stated that the '_____' _____s average. This is incorrect if '_____' is taken in the specific sense of 'arithmetic _____' as there are different types of averages: the _____, median, and mode. For instance, average house prices almost always use the median value for the average. These three types of averages are all measures of locations.

a. Standard normal distribution
b. Heteroskedastic
c. Confidence interval
d. Mean

24. _____ refer to a collection of facts usually collected as the result of experience, observation or experiment or a set of premises. This may consist of numbers, words particularly as measurements or observations of a set of variables. _____ are often viewed as a lowest level of abstraction from which information and knowledge are derived.

a. Pearson product-moment correlation coefficient
b. Mean
c. Sample size
d. Data

Chapter 8. The Concept of Measurement

25. _____ is a type of a rating scale designed to measure the connotative meaning of objects, events, and concepts. The connotations are used to derive the attitude towards the given object, event or concept.

Osgood's _____ was designed to measure the connotative meaning of concepts.

a. Factor analysis
b. Power III
c. Likert scale
d. Semantic differential

26. In algebra, a _____ is a function depending on n that associates a scalar, det(A), to an n×n square matrix A. The fundamental geometric meaning of a _____ is a scale factor for measure when A is regarded as a linear transformation. _____s are important both in calculus, where they enter the substitution rule for several variables, and in multilinear algebra.

For a fixed nonnegative integer n, there is a unique _____ function for the n×n matrices over any commutative ring R. In particular, this function exists when R is the field of real or complex numbers.

a. Package-on-Package
b. Black Friday
c. Determinant
d. Motion Picture Association of America's film-rating system

Chapter 9. Questionnaire Design

1. A _____ is a research instrument consisting of a series of questions and other prompts for the purpose of gathering information from respondents. Although they are often designed for statistical analysis of the responses, this is not always the case. The _____ was invented by Sir Francis Galton.
    a. Questionnaire
    b. Mystery shopping
    c. Mystery shoppers
    d. Market research

2. _____ a research method involving the use of questionnaires and/or statistical surveys to gather data about people and their thoughts and behaviours.
    a. T-test
    b. Control chart
    c. Z-test
    d. Survey research

3. _____ is defined by the American _____ Association as the activity, set of institutions, and processes for creating, communicating, delivering, and exchanging offerings that have value for customers, clients, partners, and society at large. The term developed from the original meaning which referred literally to going to market, as in shopping, or going to a market to sell goods or services.

    _____ practice tends to be seen as a creative industry, which includes advertising, distribution and selling.

    a. Customer acquisition management
    b. Marketing myopia
    c. Marketing
    d. Product naming

4. Consumer market research is a form of applied sociology that concentrates on understanding the behaviours, whims and preferences, of consumers in a market-based economy, and aims to understand the effects and comparative success of marketing campaigns. The field of consumer _____ as a statistical science was pioneered by Arthur Nielsen with the founding of the ACNielsen Company in 1923.

Thus _____ is the systematic and objective identification, collection, analysis, and dissemination of information for the purpose of assisting management in decision making related to the identification and solution of problems and opportunities in marketing.

Chapter 9. Questionnaire Design

a. Logit analysis
b. Marketing research
c. Marketing research process
d. Focus group

5. _____ is a telephone surveying technique in which the interviewer follows a script provided by a software application. The software is able to customize the flow of the questionnaire based on the answers provided, as well as information already known about the participant.

CATI may function in the following manner

- A computerized questionnaire is administered to respondents over the telephone.
- The interviewer sits in front of a computer screen
- Upon command, the computer dials the telephone number to be called.
- When contact is made, the interviewer reads the questions posed on the computer screen and records the respondent's answers directly into the computer.
- Interim and update reports can be compiled instantaneously, as the data are being collected.
- CATI software has built-in logic, which also enhances data accuracy.
- The program will personalize questions and control for logically incorrect answers, such as percentage answers that do not add up to 100 percent.
- The software has built-in branching logic, which will skip questions that are not applicable or will probe for more detail when warranted.

a. Computer-assisted telephone interviewing
b. 180SearchAssistant
c. Power III
d. 6-3-5 Brainwriting

6. In common law systems that rely on testimony by witnesses, a _____ is a question that suggests the answer or contains the information the examiner is looking for. For example, this question is leading:

- You were at Duffy's bar on the night of July 15, weren't you?

It suggests that the witness was at Duffy's bar on the night in question. The same question in a non-leading form would be:

- Where were you on the night of July 15?

This form of question does not suggest to the witness the answer the examiner hopes to elicit.

Chapter 9. Questionnaire Design

_____s may often be answerable with a yes or no (though not all yes-no questions are leading), while non-_____s are open-ended. Depending on the circumstances _____s can be objectionable or proper.

a. Substantive law
b. Contract price
c. Power III
d. Leading question

7. _____ is a form of assessment in which respondents are asked to select one or more choices from a list. The _____ format is most frequently used in educational testing, in market research, and in elections-- when a person chooses between multiple candidates, parties, or policies. _____ testing is particularly popular in the United States.

a. Multiple choice
b. 180SearchAssistant
c. 6-3-5 Brainwriting
d. Power III

8. A _____ is an advance video or DVD copy of a film sent to critics, awards voters, video stores (for their manager and employees), and other film industry professionals, including producers and distributors. Often, each individual _____ is sent out with distinct markings (such as a digital watermark), which allow copies of a _____ to be tracked to their source.

In 2003 the MPAA announced that they would be ceasing distribution of _____s to Academy members, citing fears of piracy.

a. Geographical indication
b. Madrid system
c. Screener
d. Trademark dilution

9. In economics, business, retail, and accounting, a _____ is the value of money that has been used up to produce something, and hence is not available for use anymore. In economics, a _____ is an alternative that is given up as a result of a decision. In business, the _____ may be one of acquisition, in which case the amount of money expended to acquire it is counted as _____.

a. Cost
b. Variable cost
c. Transaction cost
d. Fixed costs

Chapter 9. Questionnaire Design

10. _____ is the process whereby companies use cost accounting to report or control the various costs of doing business.

The term _____ is widely used in business today. Unfortunately _____ has no uniform definition.

    a. Power III
    b. 180SearchAssistant
    c. Cost management
    d. Customer profitability

11. The Oxford University Press defines _____ as 'marketing on a worldwide scale reconciling or taking commercial advantage of global operational differences, similarities and opportunities in order to meet global objectives.' Oxford University Press' Glossary of Marketing Terms.

Here are three reasons for the shift from domestic to _____ as given by the authors of the textbook, _____ Management--3rd Edition by Masaaki Kotabe and Kristiaan Helsen, 2004.

One of the product categories in which global competition has been easy to track is in U.S. automotive sales.

    a. Global marketing
    b. Digital marketing
    c. Guerrilla Marketing
    d. Diversity marketing

12. _____ is either an activity of a living being (such as a human), consisting of receiving knowledge of the outside world through the senses, or the recording of data using scientific instruments. The term may also refer to any datum collected during this activity.

The scientific method requires _____s of nature to formulate and test hypotheses.

    a. ACNielsen
    b. Observation
    c. AMAX
    d. ADTECH

13. _____ are used to collect quantitative information about items in a population. Surveys of human populations and institutions are common in political polling and government, health, social science and marketing research. A survey may focus on opinions or factual information depending on its purpose, and many surveys involve administering questions to individuals.

a. Gross Margin Return on Inventory Investment
b. Convergent
c. BeyondROI
d. Statistical surveys

14. _____, fundamental research (sometimes pure research), is research carried out to increase understanding of fundamental principles. Many times the end results have no direct or immediate commercial benefits, which is to say that _____ can be thought of as arising out of pure curiosity. However, in the long term it is the basis for many commercial products and applied research.
   a. Basic research
   b. Reference value
   c. Response rate
   d. Power III

15. _____ refer to a collection of facts usually collected as the result of experience, observation or experiment or a set of premises. This may consist of numbers, words particularly as measurements or observations of a set of variables. _____ are often viewed as a lowest level of abstraction from which information and knowledge are derived.
   a. Data
   b. Sample size
   c. Mean
   d. Pearson product-moment correlation coefficient

16. _____ is a term used to describe a process of preparing and collecting data - for example as part of a process improvement or similar project.

_____ usually takes place early on in an improvement project, and is often formalised through a _____ Plan which often contains the following activity.

   1. Pre collection activity - Agree goals, target data, definitions, methods
   2. Collection - _____
   3. Present Findings - usually involves some form of sorting analysis and/or presentation.

Chapter 9. Questionnaire Design

A formal _____ process is necessary as it ensures that data gathered is both defined and accurate and that subsequent decisions based on arguments embodied in the findings are valid. The process provides both a baseline from which to measure from and in certain cases a target on what to improve. Types of _____ 1-By mail questionnaires 2-By personal interview

- Six sigma
- Sampling (statistics)

a. 180SearchAssistant
b. Power III
c. 6-3-5 Brainwriting
d. Data collection

Chapter 10. Basic Sampling Issues

1. _____ is that part of statistical practice concerned with the selection of individual observations intended to yield some knowledge about a population of concern, especially for the purposes of statistical inference. Each observation measures one or more properties (weight, location, etc.) of an observable entity enumerated to distinguish objects or individuals.
   a. Sampling
   b. Sports Marketing Group
   c. AStore
   d. Richard Buckminster 'Bucky' Fuller

2. A _____ is an advance video or DVD copy of a film sent to critics, awards voters, video stores (for their manager and employees), and other film industry professionals, including producers and distributors. Often, each individual _____ is sent out with distinct markings (such as a digital watermark), which allow copies of a _____ to be tracked to their source.

   In 2003 the MPAA announced that they would be ceasing distribution of _____s to Academy members, citing fears of piracy.

   a. Geographical indication
   b. Trademark dilution
   c. Madrid system
   d. Screener

3. _____s are errors in measurement that lead to measured values being inconsistent when repeated measures of a constant attribute or quantity are taken. The word random indicates that they are inherently unpredictable, and have null expected value, namely, they are scattered about the true value, and tend to have null arithmetic mean when a measurement is repeated several times with the same instrument. All measurements are prone to _____.
   a. Power III
   b. Systematic error
   c. 180SearchAssistant
   d. Random error

4. _____ is a way of expressing knowledge or belief that an event will occur or has occurred. In mathematics the concept has been given an exact meaning in _____ theory, that is used extensively in such areas of study as mathematics, statistics, finance, gambling, science, and philosophy to draw conclusions about the likelihood of potential events and the underlying mechanics of complex systems.
   a. Linear regression
   b. Heteroskedastic
   c. Data
   d. Probability

Chapter 10. Basic Sampling Issues

5. A sample is a subject chosen from a population for investigation. A _____ is one chosen by a method involving an unpredictable component. Random sampling can also refer to taking a number of independent observations from the same probability distribution, without involving any real population.
   a. Selection bias
   b. Power III
   c. 180SearchAssistant
   d. Random sample

6. The '_____' is an expression which typically refers to the theory of scale types developed by the Harvard psychologist Stanley Smith Stevens In this article Stevens claimed that all measurement in science was conducted using four different types of numerical scales which he called 'nominal', 'ordinal', 'interval' and 'ratio'.
   a. 6-3-5 Brainwriting
   b. Levels of measurement
   c. Power III
   d. 180SearchAssistant

7. In statistics, _____ or estimation error is the error caused by observing a sample instead of the whole population.

   An estimate of a quantity of interest, such as an average or percentage, will generally be subject to sample-to-sample variation. These variations in the possible sample values of a statistic can theoretically be expressed as _____s, although in practice the exact _____ is typically unknown.

   a. Sampling error
   b. Power III
   c. Varimax rotation
   d. Two-tailed test

8. _____ is the difference between a measured value of quantity and its true value. In statistics, an error is not a 'mistake'. Variability is an inherent part of things being measured and of the measurement process.
   a. Observational error
   b. AMAX
   c. ADTECH
   d. ACNielsen

9. _____ is a statistical method involving the selection of elements from an ordered sampling frame. The most common form of _____ is an equal-probability method, in which every k^{th} element in the frame is selected, where k, the sampling interval (sometimes known as the 'skip'), is calculated as:

Chapter 10. Basic Sampling Issues

sample size (n) = population size (N) /k

Using this procedure each element in the population has a known and equal probability of selection. This makes _____ functionally similar to simple random sampling.

a. Selection bias
b. Systematic sampling
c. 180SearchAssistant
d. Power III

10. _____ is anything that is intended to save time, energy or frustration. A _____ store at a petrol station, for example, sells items that have nothing to do with gasoline/petrol, but it saves the consumer from having to go to a grocery store. '_____' is a very relative term and its meaning tends to change over time.

a. Demographic profile
b. Convenience
c. MaxDiff
d. Marketing buzz

11. A _____ is a research instrument consisting of a series of questions and other prompts for the purpose of gathering information from respondents. Although they are often designed for statistical analysis of the responses, this is not always the case. The _____ was invented by Sir Francis Galton.

a. Questionnaire
b. Mystery shoppers
c. Market research
d. Mystery shopping

12. _____ a research method involving the use of questionnaires and/or statistical surveys to gather data about people and their thoughts and behaviours.

a. T-test
b. Survey research
c. Z-test
d. Control chart

Chapter 11. Sample Size Determination 71

1. _____ is a way of expressing knowledge or belief that an event will occur or has occurred. In mathematics the concept has been given an exact meaning in _____ theory, that is used extensively in such areas of study as mathematics, statistics, finance, gambling, science, and philosophy to draw conclusions about the likelihood of potential events and the underlying mechanics of complex systems.
   a. Heteroskedastic
   b. Linear regression
   c. Probability
   d. Data

2. A sample is a subject chosen from a population for investigation. A _____ is one chosen by a method involving an unpredictable component. Random sampling can also refer to taking a number of independent observations from the same probability distribution, without involving any real population.
   a. Selection bias
   b. Power III
   c. 180SearchAssistant
   d. Random sample

3. The _____ of a statistical sample is the number of observations that constitute it. It is typically denoted n, a positive integer (natural number.)

   Typically, all else being equal, a larger _____ leads to increased precision in estimates of various properties of the population.

   a. Data
   b. Sample size
   c. Heteroskedastic
   d. Frequency distribution

4. _____ is that part of statistical practice concerned with the selection of individual observations intended to yield some knowledge about a population of concern, especially for the purposes of statistical inference. Each observation measures one or more properties (weight, location, etc.) of an observable entity enumerated to distinguish objects or individuals.
   a. AStore
   b. Sampling
   c. Richard Buckminster 'Bucky' Fuller
   d. Sports Marketing Group

5. In statistics, _____ or estimation error is the error caused by observing a sample instead of the whole population.

Chapter 11. Sample Size Determination

An estimate of a quantity of interest, such as an average or percentage, will generally be subject to sample-to-sample variation. These variations in the possible sample values of a statistic can theoretically be expressed as _____s, although in practice the exact _____ is typically unknown.

a. Power III
b. Varimax rotation
c. Two-tailed test
d. Sampling error

6. In economics, business, retail, and accounting, a _____ is the value of money that has been used up to produce something, and hence is not available for use anymore. In economics, a _____ is an alternative that is given up as a result of a decision. In business, the _____ may be one of acquisition, in which case the amount of money expended to acquire it is counted as _____.

a. Fixed costs
b. Transaction cost
c. Cost
d. Variable cost

7. _____ is the process whereby companies use cost accounting to report or control the various costs of doing business.

The term _____ is widely used in business today. Unfortunately _____ has no uniform definition.

a. Customer profitability
b. Cost management
c. Power III
d. 180SearchAssistant

8. _____ is one of the four elements of marketing mix. An organization or set of organizations (go-betweens) involved in the process of making a product or service available for use or consumption by a consumer or business user.

The other three parts of the marketing mix are product, pricing, and promotion.

a. Japan Advertising Photographers' Association
b. Comparison-Shopping agent
c. Better Living Through Chemistry
d. Distribution

Chapter 11. Sample Size Determination

9. In probability theory, the _____ states conditions under which the sum of a sufficiently large number of independent random variables, each with finite mean and variance, will be approximately normally distributed. More generally, a _____ is any of a set of weak-convergence results in probability theory. They all express the fact that a sum of many independent random variables will tend to be distributed according to one of a small set of 'attractor' (i.e. stable) distributions.
   a. 180SearchAssistant
   b. Power III
   c. 6-3-5 Brainwriting
   d. Central limit theorem

10. In statistics, _____ is a simple measure of the variability or dispersion of a data set. A low _____ indicates that the data points tend to be very close to the same value (the mean), while high _____ indicates that the data are 'spread out' over a large range of values.

   For example, the average height for adult men in the United States is about 70 inches, with a _____ of around 3 inches.

   a. Statistically significant
   b. Standard deviation
   c. Pearson product-moment correlation coefficient
   d. Z-test

11. The normal distribution is an important family of continuous probability distributions, applicable in many fields. Each member of the family may be defined by two parameters, location and scale: the mean and variance respectively. The _____ is the normal distribution with a mean of zero and a variance of one
   a. Standard score
   b. Variance
   c. Probability sampling
   d. Standard normal distribution

12. In statistics, _____ has two related meanings:

   - the arithmetic _____
   - the expected value of a random variable, which is also called the population _____.

   It is sometimes stated that the '_____' _____s average. This is incorrect if '_____' is taken in the specific sense of 'arithmetic _____' as there are different types of averages: the _____, median, and mode. For instance, average house prices almost always use the median value for the average. These three types of averages are all measures of locations.

Chapter 11. Sample Size Determination

a. Mean
b. Confidence interval
c. Heteroskedastic
d. Standard normal distribution

13. _____ is a global marketing research firm, with worldwide headquarters in New York City. Regional headquarters for North America are located in Schaumburg, IL. As of 2008, its the part of The Nielsen Company.
   a. Alloy Entertainment
   b. InfoNU
   c. E-Detailing
   d. ACNielsen

14. _____ is a form of communication that typically attempts to persuade potential customers to purchase or to consume more of a particular brand of product or service. 'While now central to the contemporary global economy and the reproduction of global production networks, it is only quite recently that _____ has been more than a marginal influence on patterns of sales and production. The formation of modern _____ was intimately bound up with the emergence of new forms of monopoly capitalism around the end of the 19th and beginning of the 20th century as one element in corporate strategies to create, organize and where possible control markets, especially for mass produced consumer goods.
   a. ADTECH
   b. AMAX
   c. Advertising
   d. ACNielsen

15. In statistics, a _____ is an interval estimate of a population parameter. Instead of estimating the parameter by a single value, an interval likely to include the parameter is given. Thus, _____s are used to indicate the reliability of an estimate.
   a. Confidence interval
   b. Linear regression
   c. T-test
   d. Sample mean

16. In population genetics and population ecology, _____ is the number of individual organisms in a population.

The effective _____ (N_e) is defined as 'the number of breeding individuals in an idealized population that would show the same amount of dispersion of allele frequencies under random genetic drift or the same amount of inbreeding as the population under consideration.' N_e is usually less than N (the absolute _____) and this has important applications in conservation genetics.

Small _____ results in increased genetic drift.

a. 180SearchAssistant
b. Power III
c. 6-3-5 Brainwriting
d. Population size

17. A _____ is a retail establishment which specializes in selling a wide range of products without a single predominant merchandise line. _____s usually sell products including apparel, furniture, appliances, electronics, and additionally select other lines of products such as paint, hardware, toiletries, cosmetics, photographic equipment, jewelery, toys, and sporting goods. Certain _____s are further classified as discount _____s.

a. Power III
b. 180SearchAssistant
c. Department Store
d. 6-3-5 Brainwriting

18. _____ is a branch of philosophy which seeks to address questions about morality, such as how a moral outcome can be achieved in a specific situation (applied _____), how moral values should be determined (normative _____), what moral values people actually abide by (descriptive _____), what the fundamental semantic, ontological, and epistemic nature of _____ or morality is (meta-_____), and how moral capacity or moral agency develops and what its nature is (moral psychology.)

Socrates was one of the first Greek philosophers to encourage both scholars and the common citizen to turn their attention from the outside world to the condition of man. In this view, Knowledge having a bearing on human life was placed highest, all other knowledge being secondary.

a. ACNielsen
b. ADTECH
c. Ethics
d. AMAX

19. _____ is defined by the American _____ Association as the activity, set of institutions, and processes for creating, communicating, delivering, and exchanging offerings that have value for customers, clients, partners, and society at large. The term developed from the original meaning which referred literally to going to market, as in shopping, or going to a market to sell goods or services.

_____ practice tends to be seen as a creative industry, which includes advertising, distribution and selling.

a. Marketing myopia
b. Customer acquisition management
c. Marketing
d. Product naming

20. Consumer market research is a form of applied sociology that concentrates on understanding the behaviours, whims and preferences, of consumers in a market-based economy, and aims to understand the effects and comparative success of marketing campaigns. The field of consumer _____ as a statistical science was pioneered by Arthur Nielsen with the founding of the ACNielsen Company in 1923.

Thus _____ is the systematic and objective identification, collection, analysis, and dissemination of information for the purpose of assisting management in decision making related to the identification and solution of problems and opportunities in marketing.

a. Focus group
b. Marketing research process
c. Logit analysis
d. Marketing research

Chapter 12. Data Processing and Fundamental Data Analysis

1. _____ refer to a collection of facts usually collected as the result of experience, observation or experiment or a set of premises. This may consist of numbers, words particularly as measurements or observations of a set of variables. _____ are often viewed as a lowest level of abstraction from which information and knowledge are derived.
   a. Data
   b. Sample size
   c. Pearson product-moment correlation coefficient
   d. Mean

2. _____ is a process of gathering, modeling, and transforming data with the goal of highlighting useful information, suggesting conclusions, and supporting decision making. _____ has multiple facets and approaches, encompassing diverse techniques under a variety of names, in different business, science, and social science domains.

   Data mining is a particular _____ technique that focuses on modeling and knowledge discovery for predictive rather than purely descriptive purposes.

   a. 6-3-5 Brainwriting
   b. Power III
   c. Data analysis
   d. 180SearchAssistant

3. _____ are used to collect quantitative information about items in a population. Surveys of human populations and institutions are common in political polling and government, health, social science and marketing research. A survey may focus on opinions or factual information depending on its purpose, and many surveys involve administering questions to individuals.
   a. Statistical surveys
   b. BeyondROI
   c. Convergent
   d. Gross Margin Return on Inventory Investment

4. A _____ is a research instrument consisting of a series of questions and other prompts for the purpose of gathering information from respondents. Although they are often designed for statistical analysis of the responses, this is not always the case. The _____ was invented by Sir Francis Galton.
   a. Mystery shopping
   b. Questionnaire
   c. Market research
   d. Mystery shoppers

5. _____ a research method involving the use of questionnaires and/or statistical surveys to gather data about people and their thoughts and behaviours.

Chapter 12. Data Processing and Fundamental Data Analysis

a. Survey research
b. T-test
c. Z-test
d. Control chart

6. _____, fundamental research (sometimes pure research), is research carried out to increase understanding of fundamental principles. Many times the end results have no direct or immediate commercial benefits, which is to say that _____ can be thought of as arising out of pure curiosity. However, in the long term it is the basis for many commercial products and applied research.
   a. Basic research
   b. Power III
   c. Response rate
   d. Reference value

7. _____ is a computer program used for statistical analysis.

_____ (originally, Statistical Package for the Social Sciences) was released in its first version in 1968 after being founded by Norman Nie and C. Hadlai Hull. Nie was then a political science postgraduate at Stanford University, and now Research Professor in the Department of Political Science at Stanford and Professor Emeritus of Political Science at the University of Chicago.

   a. 6-3-5 Brainwriting
   b. SPSS
   c. Power III
   d. 180SearchAssistant

8. _____s are used in open sentences. For instance, in the formula x + 1 = 5, x is a _____ which represents an 'unknown' number. _____s are often represented by letters of the Roman alphabet, or those of other alphabets, such as Greek, and use other special symbols.
   a. Quantitative
   b. Personalization
   c. Variable
   d. Book of business

9. _____ are used to describe the basic features of the data gathered from an experimental study in various ways. A _____ is distinguished from inductive statistics. They provide simple summaries about the sample and the measures.

a. Descriptive statistics
b. Pearson product-moment correlation coefficient
c. P-Value
d. Frequency distribution

10. In statistics, _____ has two related meanings:

- the arithmetic _____
- the expected value of a random variable, which is also called the population _____.

It is sometimes stated that the '_____' _____s average. This is incorrect if '_____' is taken in the specific sense of 'arithmetic _____' as there are different types of averages: the _____, median, and mode. For instance, average house prices almost always use the median value for the average. These three types of averages are all measures of locations.

a. Mean
b. Heteroskedastic
c. Confidence interval
d. Standard normal distribution

11. _____ is a mathematical science pertaining to the collection, analysis, interpretation or explanation, and presentation of data. It also provides tools for prediction and forecasting based on data. It is applicable to a wide variety of academic disciplines, from the natural and social sciences to the humanities, government and business.

a. Null hypothesis
b. Median
c. Type I error
d. Statistics

12. In probability theory and statistics, a _____ is described as the number separating the higher half of a sample, a population from the lower half. The _____ of a finite list of numbers can be found by arranging all the observations from lowest value to highest value and picking the middle one. If there is an even number of observations, the _____ is not unique, so one often takes the mean of the two middle values.

a. Median
b. Linear regression
c. Statistically significant
d. Frequency distribution

Chapter 12. Data Processing and Fundamental Data Analysis

13. In probability theory and statistics, _____ indicates the strength and direction of a linear relationship between two random variables. That is in contrast with the usage of the term in colloquial speech, denoting any relationship, not necessarily linear. In general statistical usage, _____ or co-relation refers to the departure of two random variables from independence.
    a. Correlation
    b. Probability
    c. Mean
    d. Frequency distribution

14. In statistics, a result is called _____ if it is unlikely to have occurred by chance. 'A _____ difference' simply means there is statistical evidence that there is a difference; it does not mean the difference is necessarily large, important, or significant in the common meaning of the word.

    The significance level of a test is a traditional frequentist statistical hypothesis testing concept.

    a. Randomization
    b. Standard deviation
    c. Statistically significant
    d. Frequency distribution

15. A set of _____ is the verbal equivalent of a graphical decision tree, which specifies class membership based on a hierarchical sequence of (contingent) decisions. Each rule in a set of _____ therefore generally takes the form of a Horn clause wherein class membership is implied by a conjunction of contingent observations.

    IF condition$_1$ AND condition$_2$ AND ...

    a. 6-3-5 Brainwriting
    b. Power III
    c. Decision rules
    d. 180SearchAssistant

16. In statistics, the terms _____ and type II error are used to describe possible errors made in a statistical decision process. In 1928, Jerzy Neyman (1894-1981) and Egon Pearson (1895-1980), both eminent statisticians, discussed the problems associated with 'deciding whether or not a particular sample may be judged as likely to have been randomly drawn from a certain population' (1928/1967, p.1): and identified 'two sources of error', namely:

    Type I (>α): reject the null-hypothesis when the null-hypothesis is true, and
    Type II (>β): fail to reject the null-hypothesis when the null-hypothesis is false

Chapter 12. Data Processing and Fundamental Data Analysis 81

In 1930, they elaborated on these two sources of error, remarking that 'in testing hypotheses two considerations must be kept in view, (1) we must be able to reduce the chance of rejecting a true hypothesis to as low a value as desired; (2) the test must be so devised that it will reject the hypothesis tested when it is likely to be false'

Scientists recognize two different sorts of error:

- Statistical error: the difference between a computed, estimated specified and inherently unpredictable fluctuations in the measurement apparatus or the system being studied.
- Systematic error: the difference between a computed, estimated specified and which, once identified, can usually be eliminated.

Statisticians speak of two significant sorts of statistical error. The context is that there is a 'null hypothesis' which corresponds to a presumed default 'state of nature', e.g., that an individual is free of disease, that an accused is innocent that is, that the individual has the disease, that the accused is guilty, or that the login candidate is an authorized user.

    a. Significance level
    b. Probability sampling
    c. Mean
    d. Type I error

17. _____ is that part of statistical practice concerned with the selection of individual observations intended to yield some knowledge about a population of concern, especially for the purposes of statistical inference. Each observation measures one or more properties (weight, location, etc.) of an observable entity enumerated to distinguish objects or individuals.

    a. Sampling
    b. AStore
    c. Richard Buckminster 'Bucky' Fuller
    d. Sports Marketing Group

18. _____ is defined by the American _____ Association as the activity, set of institutions, and processes for creating, communicating, delivering, and exchanging offerings that have value for customers, clients, partners, and society at large. The term developed from the original meaning which referred literally to going to market, as in shopping, or going to a market to sell goods or services.

_____ practice tends to be seen as a creative industry, which includes advertising, distribution and selling.

Chapter 12. Data Processing and Fundamental Data Analysis

a. Marketing
b. Marketing myopia
c. Product naming
d. Customer acquisition management

19. Consumer market research is a form of applied sociology that concentrates on understanding the behaviours, whims and preferences, of consumers in a market-based economy, and aims to understand the effects and comparative success of marketing campaigns. The field of consumer _____ as a statistical science was pioneered by Arthur Nielsen with the founding of the ACNielsen Company in 1923.

Thus _____ is the systematic and objective identification, collection, analysis, and dissemination of information for the purpose of assisting management in decision making related to the identification and solution of problems and opportunities in marketing.

a. Focus group
b. Logit analysis
c. Marketing research process
d. Marketing research

20. Human beings are also considered to be _____ because they have the ability to change raw materials into valuable _____. The term Human _____ can also be defined as the skills, energies, talents, abilities and knowledge that are used for the production of goods or the rendering of services. While taking into account human beings as _____, the following things have to be kept in mind:

- The size of the population
- The capabilities of the individuals in that population

Many _____ cannot be consumed in their original form. They have to be processed in order to change them into more usable commodities.

a. 180SearchAssistant
b. 6-3-5 Brainwriting
c. Power III
d. Resources

21. A personal and cultural _____ is a relative ethic _____, an assumption upon which implementation can be extrapolated. A _____ system is a set of consistent _____s and measures that is soo not true. A principle _____ is a foundation upon which other _____s and measures of integrity are based.

a. Supreme Court of the United States
b. Value
c. Perceptual maps
d. Package-on-Package

22. A _____ is a structured collection of records or data that is stored in a computer system. The structure is achieved by organizing the data according to a _____ model. The model in most common use today is the relational model.
    a. Database
    b. 180SearchAssistant
    c. 6-3-5 Brainwriting
    d. Power III

Chapter 13. Bivariate Correlation and Regression

1. A _____ is a collection of symbols, experiences and associations connected with a product, a service, a person or any other artifact or entity.

   _____s have become increasingly important components of culture and the economy, now being described as 'cultural accessories and personal philosophies'.

   Some people distinguish the psychological aspect of a _____ from the experiential aspect.

   a. Brandable software
   b. Store brand
   c. Brand equity
   d. Brand

2. The terms '_____' and 'independent variable' are used in similar but subtly different ways in mathematics and statistics as part of the standard terminology in those subjects. They are used to distinguish between two types of quantities being considered, separating them into those available at the start of a process and those being created by it, where the latter (_____s) are dependent on the former (independent variables.)

   In traditional calculus, a function is defined as a relation between two terms called variables because their values vary.

   a. Field experiment
   b. 180SearchAssistant
   c. Power III
   d. Dependent variable

3. _____s are used in open sentences. For instance, in the formula x + 1 = 5, x is a _____ which represents an 'unknown' number. _____s are often represented by letters of the Roman alphabet, or those of other alphabets, such as Greek, and use other special symbols.
   a. Variable
   b. Book of business
   c. Personalization
   d. Quantitative

4. In statistics, _____ is a collective name for techniques for the modeling and analysis of numerical data consisting of values of a dependent variable and of one or more independent variables The dependent variable in the regression equation is modeled as a function of the independent variables, corresponding parameters, and an error term. The error term is treated as a random variable.

a. Multicollinearity
b. Variance inflation factor
c. Stepwise regression
d. Regression analysis

5. The Oxford University Press defines _____ as 'marketing on a worldwide scale reconciling or taking commercial advantage of global operational differences, similarities and opportunities in order to meet global objectives.' Oxford University Press' Glossary of Marketing Terms.

Here are three reasons for the shift from domestic to _____ as given by the authors of the textbook, _____ Management--3rd Edition by Masaaki Kotabe and Kristiaan Helsen, 2004.

One of the product categories in which global competition has been easy to track is in U.S. automotive sales.

a. Diversity marketing
b. Guerrilla Marketing
c. Global marketing
d. Digital marketing

6. _____ is defined by the American _____ Association as the activity, set of institutions, and processes for creating, communicating, delivering, and exchanging offerings that have value for customers, clients, partners, and society at large. The term developed from the original meaning which referred literally to going to market, as in shopping, or going to a market to sell goods or services.

_____ practice tends to be seen as a creative industry, which includes advertising, distribution and selling.

a. Product naming
b. Marketing myopia
c. Customer acquisition management
d. Marketing

7. Consumer market research is a form of applied sociology that concentrates on understanding the behaviours, whims and preferences, of consumers in a market-based economy, and aims to understand the effects and comparative success of marketing campaigns. The field of consumer _____ as a statistical science was pioneered by Arthur Nielsen with the founding of the ACNielsen Company in 1923.

Thus _____ is the systematic and objective identification, collection, analysis, and dissemination of information for the purpose of assisting management in decision making related to the identification and solution of problems and opportunities in marketing.

Chapter 13. Bivariate Correlation and Regression

a. Marketing research process
b. Focus group
c. Marketing research
d. Logit analysis

8. In statistics, the _____, R^2 is used in the context of statistical models whose main purpose is the prediction of future outcomes on the basis of other related information. It is the proportion of variability in a data set that is accounted for by the statistical model. It provides a measure of how well future outcomes are likely to be predicted by the model.
    a. Variance inflation factor
    b. Regression analysis
    c. Multicollinearity
    d. Coefficient of determination

9. In statistics, _____ is a collection of statistical models, and their associated procedures, in which the observed variance is partitioned into components due to different explanatory variables. The initial techniques of the _____ were developed by the statistician and geneticist R. A. Fisher in the 1920s and 1930s, and is sometimes known as Fisher's ANOVA or Fisher's _____, due to the use of Fisher's F-distribution as part of the test of statistical significance.

There are three conceptual classes of such models:

1. Fixed-effects models assumes that the data came from normal populations which may differ only in their means. (Model 1)
2. Random effects models assume that the data describe a hierarchy of different populations whose differences are constrained by the hierarchy. (Model 2)
3. Mixed-effect models describe situations where both fixed and random effects are present. (Model 3)

In practice, there are several types of ANOVA depending on the number of treatments and the way they are applied to the subjects in the experiment:

- One-way ANOVA is used to test for differences among two or more independent groups. Typically, however, the One-way ANOVA is used to test for differences among at least three groups, since the two-group case can be covered by a T-test (Gossett, 1908.)

a. Interval estimation
b. Analysis of variance
c. Arithmetic mean
d. ACNielsen

Chapter 13. Bivariate Correlation and Regression

10. In probability theory and statistics, the _____ of a random variable, probability distribution, or sample is a measure of statistical dispersion, averaging the squared distance of its possible values from the expected value (mean.) Whereas the mean is a way to describe the location of a distribution, the _____ is a way to capture its scale or degree of being spread out. The unit of _____ is the square of the unit of the original variable.
    a. Variance
    b. Correlation
    c. Standard deviation
    d. Sample size

11. In probability theory and statistics, _____ indicates the strength and direction of a linear relationship between two random variables. That is in contrast with the usage of the term in colloquial speech, denoting any relationship, not necessarily linear. In general statistical usage, _____ or co-relation refers to the departure of two random variables from independence.
    a. Frequency distribution
    b. Mean
    c. Probability
    d. Correlation

12. _____ refer to a collection of facts usually collected as the result of experience, observation or experiment or a set of premises. This may consist of numbers, words particularly as measurements or observations of a set of variables. _____ are often viewed as a lowest level of abstraction from which information and knowledge are derived.
    a. Sample size
    b. Mean
    c. Pearson product-moment correlation coefficient
    d. Data

13. The _____ is a standardized test for college admissions in the United States. The SAT is owned, published, and developed by the College Board, a non-profit organization in the United States, and was once developed, published, and scored by the Educational Testing Service (ETS.) ETS now administers the exam.
    a. SAT Reasoning Test
    b. 6-3-5 Brainwriting
    c. Power III
    d. 180SearchAssistant

Chapter 14. Communicating the Research Results

1. _____s are used in open sentences. For instance, in the formula x + 1 = 5, x is a _____ which represents an 'unknown' number. _____s are often represented by letters of the Roman alphabet, or those of other alphabets, such as Greek, and use other special symbols.
   a. Book of business
   b. Quantitative
   c. Variable
   d. Personalization

2. _____ in organizations and public policy is both the organizational process of creating and maintaining a plan; and the psychological process of thinking about the activities required to create a desired goal on some scale. As such, it is a fundamental property of intelligent behavior. This thought process is essential to the creation and refinement of a plan, or integration of it with other plans, that is, it combines forecasting of developments with the preparation of scenarios of how to react to them.
   a. Planning
   b. 180SearchAssistant
   c. Power III
   d. 6-3-5 Brainwriting

3. _____ is an organization's process of defining its strategy and making decisions on allocating its resources to pursue this strategy, including its capital and people. Various business analysis techniques can be used in _____, including SWOT analysis (Strengths, Weaknesses, Opportunities, and Threats) and PEST analysis (Political, Economic, Social, and Technological analysis) or STEER analysis involving Socio-cultural, Technological, Economic, Ecological, and Regulatory factors and EPISTEL (Environment, Political, Informatic, Social, Technological, Economic and Legal)

_____ is the formal consideration of an organization's future course. All _____ deals with at least one of three key questions:

   1. 'What do we do?'
   2. 'For whom do we do it?'
   3. 'How do we excel?'

In business _____, the third question is better phrased 'How can we beat or avoid competition?'. (Bradford and Duncan, page 1.)

   a. 6-3-5 Brainwriting
   b. Strategic Planning
   c. Power III
   d. 180SearchAssistant

Chapter 14. Communicating the Research Results

4. _____ is defined by the American _____ Association as the activity, set of institutions, and processes for creating, communicating, delivering, and exchanging offerings that have value for customers, clients, partners, and society at large. The term developed from the original meaning which referred literally to going to market, as in shopping, or going to a market to sell goods or services.

_____ practice tends to be seen as a creative industry, which includes advertising, distribution and selling.

   a. Marketing
   b. Product naming
   c. Marketing myopia
   d. Customer acquisition management

5. Consumer market research is a form of applied sociology that concentrates on understanding the behaviours, whims and preferences, of consumers in a market-based economy, and aims to understand the effects and comparative success of marketing campaigns. The field of consumer _____ as a statistical science was pioneered by Arthur Nielsen with the founding of the ACNielsen Company in 1923.

Thus _____ is the systematic and objective identification, collection, analysis, and dissemination of information for the purpose of assisting management in decision making related to the identification and solution of problems and opportunities in marketing.

   a. Marketing research process
   b. Focus group
   c. Logit analysis
   d. Marketing research

6. _____ is either an activity of a living being (such as a human), consisting of receiving knowledge of the outside world through the senses, or the recording of data using scientific instruments. The term may also refer to any datum collected during this activity.

The scientific method requires _____s of nature to formulate and test hypotheses.

   a. AMAX
   b. ADTECH
   c. Observation
   d. ACNielsen

7. _____ a research method involving the use of questionnaires and/or statistical surveys to gather data about people and their thoughts and behaviours.

a. Control chart
b. T-test
c. Z-test
d. Survey research

8. The _____ is a professional association for marketers. As of 2008 it had approximately 40,000 members. There are collegiate chapters on 250 campuses.
   a. ADTECH
   b. ACNielsen
   c. AMAX
   d. American Marketing Association

Chapter 15. Managing Marketing Research and Research Ethics 91

1. _____ is defined by the American _____ Association as the activity, set of institutions, and processes for creating, communicating, delivering, and exchanging offerings that have value for customers, clients, partners, and society at large. The term developed from the original meaning which referred literally to going to market, as in shopping, or going to a market to sell goods or services.

_____ practice tends to be seen as a creative industry, which includes advertising, distribution and selling.

   a. Marketing myopia
   b. Customer acquisition management
   c. Product naming
   d. Marketing

2. Consumer market research is a form of applied sociology that concentrates on understanding the behaviours, whims and preferences, of consumers in a market-based economy, and aims to understand the effects and comparative success of marketing campaigns. The field of consumer _____ as a statistical science was pioneered by Arthur Nielsen with the founding of the ACNielsen Company in 1923.

Thus _____ is the systematic and objective identification, collection, analysis, and dissemination of information for the purpose of assisting management in decision making related to the identification and solution of problems and opportunities in marketing.

   a. Logit analysis
   b. Marketing research
   c. Marketing research process
   d. Focus group

3. _____ is either an activity of a living being (such as a human), consisting of receiving knowledge of the outside world through the senses, or the recording of data using scientific instruments. The term may also refer to any datum collected during this activity.

The scientific method requires _____s of nature to formulate and test hypotheses.

   a. AMAX
   b. ACNielsen
   c. ADTECH
   d. Observation

4. _____ a research method involving the use of questionnaires and/or statistical surveys to gather data about people and their thoughts and behaviours.

a. T-test
b. Control chart
c. Z-test
d. Survey research

5. _____ is a branch of philosophy which seeks to address questions about morality, such as how a moral outcome can be achieved in a specific situation (applied _____), how moral values should be determined (normative _____), what moral values people actually abide by (descriptive _____), what the fundamental semantic, ontological, and epistemic nature of _____ or morality is (meta-_____), and how moral capacity or moral agency develops and what its nature is (moral psychology.)

Socrates was one of the first Greek philosophers to encourage both scholars and the common citizen to turn their attention from the outside world to the condition of man. In this view, Knowledge having a bearing on human life was placed highest, all other knowledge being secondary.

a. Ethics
b. AMAX
c. ACNielsen
d. ADTECH

6. A supply chain is the system of organizations, people, technology, activities, information and resources involved in moving a product or service from _____ to customer. Supply chain activities transform natural resources, raw materials and components into a finished product that is delivered to the end customer. In sophisticated supply chain systems, used products may re-enter the supply chain at any point where residual value is recyclable.
a. Product line extension
b. Rebate
c. Bringin' Home the Oil
d. Supplier

7. _____ refers to a range of skills, tools, and techniques utilized to accomplish specific tasks, projects and goals. This set encompass a wide scope of activities, and these include planning, setting goals, delegation, analysis of time spent, monitoring, organizing, scheduling, and prioritizing. Initially _____ referred to just business or work activities, but eventually the term broadened to include personal activities also.
a. Business plan
b. Goal setting
c. Digital strategy
d. Time management

Chapter 15. Managing Marketing Research and Research Ethics

8. In economics, business, retail, and accounting, a _____ is the value of money that has been used up to produce something, and hence is not available for use anymore. In economics, a _____ is an alternative that is given up as a result of a decision. In business, the _____ may be one of acquisition, in which case the amount of money expended to acquire it is counted as _____.
    a. Transaction cost
    b. Fixed costs
    c. Cost
    d. Variable cost

9. _____ is the process whereby companies use cost accounting to report or control the various costs of doing business. The term _____ is widely used in business today. Unfortunately _____ has no uniform definition.

    a. Cost management
    b. Customer profitability
    c. Power III
    d. 180SearchAssistant

10. _____ refer to a collection of facts usually collected as the result of experience, observation or experiment or a set of premises. This may consist of numbers, words particularly as measurements or observations of a set of variables. _____ are often viewed as a lowest level of abstraction from which information and knowledge are derived.
    a. Sample size
    b. Mean
    c. Pearson product-moment correlation coefficient
    d. Data

11. _____ is one of the four Ps of the marketing mix. The other three aspects are product, promotion, and place. It is also a key variable in microeconomic price allocation theory.
    a. Competitor indexing
    b. Relationship based pricing
    c. Price
    d. Pricing

12. A _____ is a type of wholesale merchant business that buys goods and bulk products from importers, other wholesalers and then sells to retailers. _____s can deal in any commodity destined for the retail market. Typical categories are food, lumber, hardware, fuel, and textiles.

a. Jobbing house
b. Chief privacy officer
c. Tacit collusion
d. Refusal to deal

13. _____ is an advertisement in which a particular product specifically mentions a competitor by name for the express purpose of showing why the competitor is inferior to the product naming it.

This should not be confused with parody advertisements, where a fictional product is being advertised for the purpose of poking fun at the particular advertisement, nor should it be confused with the use of a coined brand name for the purpose of comparing the product without actually naming an actual competitor. ('Wikipedia tastes better and is less filling than the Encyclopedia Galactica.')

In the 1980s, during what has been referred to as the cola wars, soft-drink manufacturer Pepsi ran a series of advertisements where people, caught on hidden camera, in a blind taste test, chose Pepsi over rival Coca-Cola.

a. Comparative advertising
b. Heavy-up
c. Cost per conversion
d. GL-70

14. _____ is the ability of an individual or group to seclude themselves or information about themselves and thereby reveal themselves selectively. The boundaries and content of what is considered private differ among cultures and individuals, but share basic common themes. _____ is sometimes related to anonymity, the wish to remain unnoticed or unidentified in the public realm.

a. Power III
b. 6-3-5 Brainwriting
c. 180SearchAssistant
d. Privacy

15. _____ is a broad label that refers to any individuals or households that use goods and services generated within the economy. The concept of a _____ is used in different contexts, so that the usage and significance of the term may vary.

A _____ is a person who uses any product or service.

a. 180SearchAssistant
b. 6-3-5 Brainwriting
c. Power III
d. Consumer

16. _____ is a form of communication that typically attempts to persuade potential customers to purchase or to consume more of a particular brand of product or service. 'While now central to the contemporary global economy and the reproduction of global production networks, it is only quite recently that _____ has been more than a marginal influence on patterns of sales and production. The formation of modern _____ was intimately bound up with the emergence of new forms of monopoly capitalism around the end of the 19th and beginning of the 20th century as one element in corporate strategies to create, organize and where possible control markets, especially for mass produced consumer goods.
   a. ADTECH
   b. ACNielsen
   c. AMAX
   d. Advertising

17. _____ is a specialized form of marketing research conducted to improve the efficiency of advertising. According to MarketConscious.com, 'It may focus on a specific ad or campaign, or may be directed at a more general understanding of how advertising works or how consumers use the information in advertising. It can entail a variety of research approaches, including psychological, sociological, economic, and other perspectives.'

1879 - N.W. Ayer conducts custom research in an attempt to win the advertising business of Nichols-Shepard Co., a manufacturer of agricultural machinery.

   a. Electrolux
   b. American Medical Association
   c. INVISTA
   d. Advertising Research

18. The _____ is a nonprofit industry association for creating, aggregating, synthesizing and sharing the knowledge in the fields of advertising and media. It was founded in 1936 by the Association of National Advertisers and the American Association of Advertising Agencies. Its stated mission is to improve the practice of advertising, marketing and media research in pursuit of more effective marketing and advertising communications.
   a. Intent scale translation
   b. Advertising Research Foundation
   c. IDDEA
   d. ACNielsen

Chapter 15. Managing Marketing Research and Research Ethics

19. The business terms _____ and pull originated in the logistic and supply chain management, but are also widely used in marketing.

A _____-pull-system in business describes the move of a product or information between two subjects. On markets the consumers usually 'pulls' the goods or information they demand for their needs, while the offerers or suppliers '_____es' them toward the consumers.

a. Push
b. Manufacturers' representatives
c. Gold Key Matching Service
d. Completely randomized designs

20. A _____ is a political campaign technique in which an individual or organization attempts to influence or alter the view of respondents under the guise of conducting a poll. In a _____, large numbers of respondents are contacted, and little or no effort is made to collect and analyze response data. Instead, the _____ is a form of telemarketing-based propaganda and rumor mongering, masquerading as a poll.

a. 180SearchAssistant
b. 6-3-5 Brainwriting
c. Power III
d. Push poll

21. _____ refers to the confirmation of certain characteristics of an object, person, or organization. This confirmation is often, but not always, provided by some form of external review, education, or assessment. One of the most common types of _____ in modern society is professional _____, where a person is certified as being able to competently complete a job or task, usually by the passing of an examination.

a. 6-3-5 Brainwriting
b. 180SearchAssistant
c. Power III
d. Certification

22. The verb _____ or grant _____ means to give permission. The noun _____ refers to that permission as well as to the document memorializing that permission. _____ may be granted by a party to another party as an element of an agreement between those parties.

a. 6-3-5 Brainwriting
b. 180SearchAssistant
c. License
d. Power III

ANSWER KEY

Chapter 1
1. b   2. d   3. d   4. c   5. d   6. d   7. c   8. d   9. c   10. a
11. b 12. d 13. b 14. d 15. a 16. d 17. b

Chapter 2
1. a   2. b   3. d   4. b   5. d   6. a   7. b   8. d   9. c   10. d
11. b 12. a 13. b 14. d 15. b 16. d 17. a 18. b 19. d 20. d

Chapter 3
1. d   2. b   3. b   4. d   5. d   6. d   7. d   8. a   9. d   10. b
11. b 12. d 13. c 14. a 15. d 16. a 17. a 18. a 19. b 20. a
21. b 22. a 23. d 24. a 25. a 26. a

Chapter 4
1. b   2. a   3. c   4. d   5. b   6. b   7. a   8. a   9. b   10. d
11. c 12. a 13. d 14. c 15. a 16. d 17. a 18. d 19. d 20. d
21. c

Chapter 5
1. c   2. a   3. a   4. d   5. d   6. d   7. d   8. c   9. a   10. d
11. c 12. a 13. d 14. d 15. d 16. c 17. d 18. c 19. d 20. b
21. d 22. d 23. c 24. b 25. c 26. d 27. b 28. d 29. b 30. d
31. a 32. b 33. d 34. d

Chapter 6
1. d   2. d   3. c   4. d   5. d   6. d   7. b   8. d   9. c   10. a
11. a 12. d 13. d 14. d 15. c 16. d 17. c 18. d 19. d 20. a
21. c 22. d 23. d 24. a 25. d 26. d

Chapter 7
1. a   2. d   3. d   4. a   5. d   6. d   7. d   8. a   9. b   10. b
11. d 12. c 13. b 14. b 15. d 16. a 17. d 18. b 19. a 20. d
21. d

Chapter 8
1. b   2. b   3. d   4. b   5. b   6. d   7. d   8. d   9. c   10. c
11. a 12. d 13. d 14. d 15. a 16. d 17. b 18. d 19. d 20. d
21. c 22. d 23. d 24. d 25. d 26. c

Chapter 9
1. a   2. d   3. c   4. b   5. a   6. d   7. a   8. c   9. a   10. c
11. a 12. b 13. d 14. a 15. a 16. d

Chapter 10
1. a   2. d   3. d   4. d   5. d   6. b   7. a   8. a   9. b   10. b
11. a 12. b

Chapter 11

| 1. c | 2. d | 3. b | 4. b | 5. d | 6. c | 7. b | 8. d | 9. d | 10. b |
| 11. d | 12. a | 13. d | 14. c | 15. a | 16. d | 17. c | 18. c | 19. c | 20. d |

Chapter 12

1. a	2. c	3. a	4. b	5. a	6. a	7. b	8. c	9. a	10. a
11. d	12. a	13. a	14. c	15. c	16. d	17. a	18. a	19. d	20. d
21. b	22. a								

Chapter 13

| 1. d | 2. d | 3. a | 4. d | 5. c | 6. d | 7. c | 8. d | 9. b | 10. a |
| 11. d | 12. d | 13. a | | | | | | | |

Chapter 14

| 1. c | 2. a | 3. b | 4. a | 5. d | 6. c | 7. d | 8. d |

Chapter 15

1. d	2. b	3. d	4. d	5. a	6. d	7. d	8. c	9. a	10. d
11. d	12. a	13. a	14. d	15. d	16. d	17. d	18. b	19. a	20. d
21. d	22. c								

www.ingramcontent.com/pod-product-compliance
Lightning Source LLC
Chambersburg PA
CBHW081846230426

43669CB00018B/2837